SOMEWHERE OVER THE SQUARE

AN AERIAL ANALYSIS OF URBAN DEVELOPMENT

Translation: Mihai Murariu
Lecturer: Dan Bora
Proofreading: Alyssa Grossman
Graphic Design and Layout: Cătălin D. Constantin

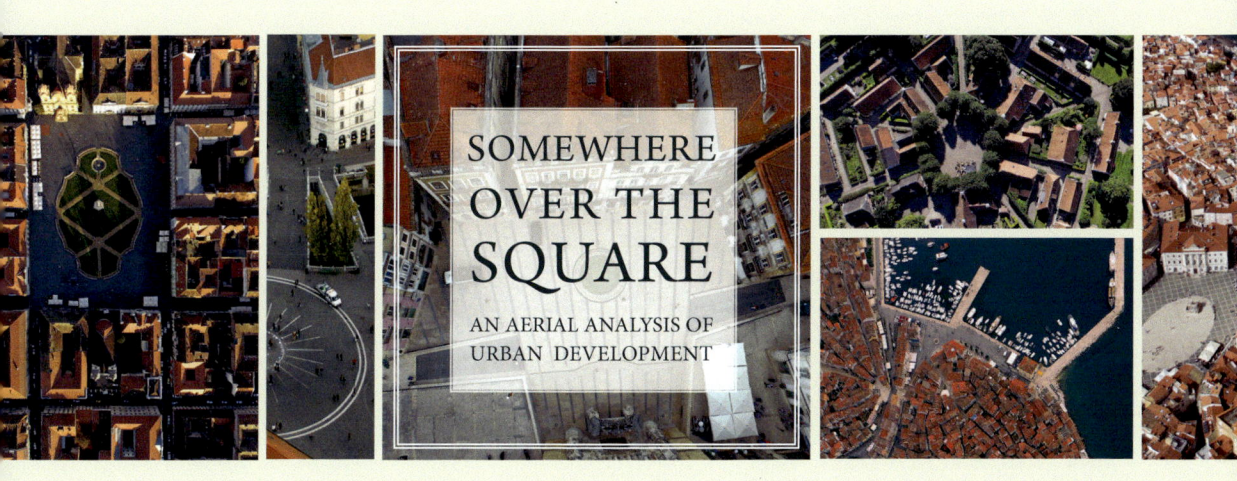

Somewhere Over the Square

An Aerial Analysis of Urban Development

text and photography by

CĂTĂLIN D. CONSTANTIN

PETER LANG

Oxford · Bern · Berlin · Bruxelles · New York · Wien

Bibliographic information published by Die Deutsche Nationalbibliothek.
Die Deutsche Nationalbibliothek lists this publication in the Deutsche Nationalbibliografie;
detailed bibliographic data are available on the Internet at http://dnb.d-nb.de/.

A catalogue record for this book is available from the British Library.

Library of Congress Cataloging-in-Publication Data

Names: Constantin, Cătălin D., author.
Title: Somewhere over the square : an aerial analysis of urban development
   / Cătălin D. Constantin.
Description: Oxford ; New York : Peter Lang, [2021] | Includes
   bibliographical references and index.
Identifiers: LCCN 2021014929 (print) | LCCN 2021014930 (ebook) |
   ISBN 9781800794979 (paperback) | ISBN 9781800794986 (ebook) |
   ISBN 9781800794993 (epub)
Subjects: LCSH: Plazas--Europe--Pictorial works. | Public spaces--Europe. |
   Aerial photography in city planning.
Classification: LCC NA9070 .C656 2021 (print) | LCC NA9070 (ebook) |
   DDC 711/.55094--dc23
LC record available at https://lccn.loc.gov/2021014929
LC ebook record available at https://lccn.loc.gov/2021014930

Original version of the book was published in English, 2020, by Peter Pan ART, Bucharest,
Romania, ISBN 978-606-95000-1-9. Part of the content was initially included in the volume
Orașe în rezumat. Piețe din Europa și istoriile lor (*Summarising Cities. European Squares and
their Histories*), 2017, published in Romanian language by Peter Pan Art in co-edition with Ion
Mincu University Publishing House, ISBN: 978-606-92300-4-6.

Cover image: Masarykovo náměstí, Nový Jičín, Czech Republic

ISBN 978-1-80079-497-9 (print)
ISBN 978-1-80079-498-6 (ePDF)
ISBN 978-1-80079-499-3 (ePub)

© Peter Lang Group AG 2021 for the present edition
Published by Peter Lang Ltd, International Academic Publishers,
52 St Giles, Oxford, OX1 3LU, United Kingdom
oxford@peterlang.com, www.peterlang.com

Cătălin D. Constantin has asserted his right under the Copyright, Designs and Patents Act, 1988,
to be identified as Author of this Work.

All rights reserved.
All parts of this publication are protected by copyright.
Any utilisation outside the strict limits of the copyright law, without the
permission of the publisher, is forbidden and liable to prosecution.
This applies in particular to reproductions, translations, microfilming,
and storage and processing in electronic retrieval systems.

This publication has been peer reviewed.

EUROPEAN SQUARES

and their histories

In European cities, the square is the most important public space. The main roads of a city lead to the its square, where one finds the most important buildings, statues, and other artifacts. A European city square is the sum of its historical, architectural, cultural and social parts; it is a palimpsest that reveals many histories – if one knows how to read it. In this respect, the square holds a place of privilege among the various types of urban spaces.

The physical spaces of urban squares are the main theme of this book. Aerial photographs taken with a professional drone offer a different perspective on the European square. This might seem like a bold proposition, but it should be first and foremost taken literally. One cannot see the entirety of a square from street level, except perhaps in some cities where climbing the creaky stairs of a cathedral tower offers a broader vista from a higher vantage point. The question of altitude may seem like a banal starting point, but it has important visual consequences, particularly for understanding the square as a historical and cultural phenomenon. These bird's eye view images present a successful overlap of technical and artistic languages, revealing something we might have merely intuited until now: a deeper structure. And so, there is a chance that our figurative perspective on squares will also be revised. Despite their differences, squares have much in common, from their broader functions to the ways in which they reflect aspects of people's lives. And all squares have something obvious in common: they do not exist in isolation – they are located within a settlement. Looking at how a square relates to its surroundings is the clearest method for defining its anthropological and visual nature. Whether it evolved organically, or was built according to planned diagrams and grids, the structure of a city presents a fundamental tension between the space of the square and space outside it. This is immediately visible only from above: open space versus closed space, a space of motion versus a stationary space. In *Cities for People*, Jan Gehl defines the difference between the two parts of the city: 'While streets transmit the idea of motion – "move along, please!" – on a psychological level, squares suggest leisure. The circulation spaces ask us to "move, move!" while the square says: "let us stop and see what is going on here!" As basic units of a human scale, the feet and the eyes have left indelible marks on the history of urban planning. The basic units of city architecture are spaces of motion – streets – and of perception – squares.'

To a certain degree the selection of squares to be presented was subjective, however these squares are also among the best examples I was able to find to illustrate the historical, conservation, and urbanistic arguments presented in this book. I relentlessly favoured the lesser known and less travelled squares, although some famous squares do appear in the following pages. A number of European countries significant to the study of squares are missing for a technical reason: drone photography is not legally possible and, in the meantime, in many of the countries where I had taken images, drone photography has become restricted for legal reasons. The ninety-nine squares, many relatively unknown, which comprise this book barely begin to scratch the surface of this topic. For the hundredth square, I invite you, the reader, to round off our walk by including your own favourite.

EUROPEAN SQUARES
and their histories

Pienza, Italy
Piazza Pio II

Pope Pius II loved his hometown greatly and wished to transform it into a concrete illustration of his theories about the 'ideal city'.

The area is not large, yet the illusion of space is created through its shape and the design of the pavement. The square is dominated by the façade of a Cathedral, built along the smaller side of the trapezoid, so as not to overwhelm the square. The Pope wished to build a city of human, rather than monumental, dimensions. Inspired by Austrian Cathedrals that were bathed in natural light, the Pope asked that this church not respect the traditional east – west alignment, but be set in such a way that the sun would pour in from the southern windows. The church is aligned with the top of Mount Amiata, an extinct volcano. Its peak is visible from the southern windows of the church, though it is not visible from the square. This leads to an interesting reversal of perception: the interior of the church feels like a wide space that opens out to the landscape, while the square allows limited access to its surroundings, and instead feels like an interior space. At the centre of the square is a travertine circle, and the distance between the circle and the door of the church is equal to the distance between the base of the church and the *occhio*, a typical round window on the façade of the church. This is not the only 'coincidence,' for the square respects a geometry based on the numbers 3, 5, and 9. Moreover, in the early 2000s it was found that the shadow of the Cathedral aligns perfectly with the grid of the pavement at particular moments in time, specifically, eleven days after the solar equinox.

Gubbio, Italy
Piazza Grande

Also known as the 'City of Silence', Gubbio was built on the forested side of a mountain, rather than its summit, as opposed to most cities in central Italy with Etruscan origins. Gubbio holds the title of the most beautiful citadel in Europe. The layout of this settlement, with its high towers and unexpectedly wide medieval streets, is theatrical and dramatic, with few squares surpassing the Piazza Grande de la Gubbio.

The citadel consists of five main streets, each one higher than the next, all converging in a steep incline. In the middle, one finds the Piazza Grande. Archways support the platform of the square, which on one side opens out to the vast landscape of the valley. The square is flanked by the Palazzo dei Consoli and the Palazzo Pretoria. The fourth side is a classical order, with the climb continuing towards the Cathedral and the Ducal Palace.

Todi, Italy
Piazza del Popolo, Piazza Garibaldi

Todi has three rows of fortified precincts. Following them towards the town's interior, one climbs towards its square and descends into history, crossing medieval, Roman and Etruscan walls. The square stands on the site of an old Roman *forum*, just as the Cathedral, which borders the square and some steep steps, stands on the site of a temple to Jupiter. The Piazza del Popolo of Todi, a closed space dominated by massive crenellated buildings, conveys, along with its fortifications, a strong sense of protection. It is often cited in historical studies as the most convincing example of a medieval square. It is certainly beautiful and impressive. In the neighbouring Garibaldi Square, one crosses through a narrow passage that offers an unexpected surprise when it comes to the structure of the town. It shows the exact opposite: a side that is entirely open to the Umbrian hills.

Vicenza, Italy

Piazza dei Signori, Piazza delle Biade, Piazza delle Erbe, Piazzetta Palladio

The central square of Vicenza is one of the most beautiful in northern Italy, unfolding in close connection with the *Basilica Palladiana*. It is not actually a single square, but rather a system formed by three larger squares and one smaller one on each side of the building, with the Piazza dei Signori – originally a Roman *forum* – holding the main role.

The square's horizontal landscape is counterbalanced by the vertical Torre Bissara, 82 meters tall and dating from 1174. Two columns, one with a statue of Christ and one with the lion of Saint Mark, delineate the border with the Piazza delle Biade. The *Basilica Palladiana* must be understood as a public space and as part of the square, not least because one may pass through its colonnade from the Piazza dei Signori to the Piazza delle Erbe. The success of this type of square is due to the fact that each element maintains its individuality, yet also communicates with the neighbouring spaces in a perfectly articulate manner.

Brescia, Italy
Piazza Paolo VI, Piazza della Loggia

Piazza Paolo VI is Brescia's main and largest square, part of a greater square system. It dates from the medieval period. Here one finds the Duomo Vecchio and the Duomo Nuovo, as well as Il Broletto, the city hall building. But the most beautiful of the squares in Brescia

is the neighbouring one, Piazza della Loggia. Its origins date back to the Renaissance, when, in 1489, work on the Loggia began under Filippo Grassi, in the most authentic Venetian style. All of the buildings in the square are its visual subordinates, mirroring its arch. On the opposite side, one notices the Torre dell'Orologio, whose colonnade ensures the transition towards Piazza Paolo VI. The astronomical clock in the tower dates from 1546. Piazza della Loggia holds three of the four 'talking statues' of Brescia, where the inhabitants voice their grievances about the ways in which the city is governed by leaving notes on these statues.

Pitigliano, Italy
Piazza San Gregorio VII

Pitigliano is a little-known, minor settlement in the south of Tuscany. It has Etruscan origins and is spectacularly built on volcanic tuff in which a number of tunnels and wine cellars have been dug over the ages. The space is protective, yet very narrow. With its views from up high, this practical urban structure is all the more remarkable. Its longitudinal streets, three in total, all lead towards its small, stunningly beautiful square.

Arezzo, Italy
Piazza Grande

Many of the city squares in central Italy sit at an angle, as they are situated on hilltops. Piazza Grande in Arezzo is probably the steepest of them all. The visual effect is spectacular, as the square's incline creates the illusion of a space that becomes either deeper or smaller, with side buildings that become either closer or further away, depending on the vantage point. The origins of this square are medieval. In the 13th century, Piazza Grande was a trading centre for agricultural produce from the surrounding villages. In the 16th century, the square was modified and became the community centre. Among its defining buildings, one must mention the Palazzo delle Logge, built in 1573, with its beautiful colonnade. On the first Sunday of each month, this square hosts an antiquarian fair.

Città di Castello, Italy
Piazza Gabriotti, Piazza Matteotti

Città di Castello is located in an ancient Umbrian settlement, on the fertile banks of the Tiber. The town, maintaining a large part of the buildings raised during its period of flourishing, is unusual in that it has two central squares. Equally important throughout the town's history, Piazza Gabriotti and Piazza Matteotti, once called Piazza delle Donne and Piazza Vitelli, were known by the locals as Upper Square and Lower Square. The cathedral, found in Lower Square, has a cylindrical campanile and bears the name of a local bishop, San Florido, who was sanctified and seen as a protector of the town. In the 6th century, San Florido supported the rebuilding of the settlement after the destruction by the Ostrogoths. The City Hall dates from the 14th century and is the work of Angelo da Orvieto, who built the Palazzo del Podestà in the neighbouring square. The Torre civica is the symbol of communal power.

Lucca, Italy
Piazza dell'Anfiteatro

The oval square in Lucca is the result of a special continuity. This was the location of a Roman amphitheatre whose foundations were taken over by the current square. The old pavement of the amphitheatre can be found two to three meters below that of the square. Four entrances lead to the Piazza dell'Anfiteatro, one of them dating from Antiquity, with the square's oval shape perceptible from not only within the square but also from outside it, where the surrounding Via Anfiteatro street mirrors its shape. The buildings along the square all have curved façades and stand at different heights due to the different periods of their construction. The result, however, is harmonious, with these vertical irregularities tempering the geometrically regular shape of the square.

In place of the 54 Roman arches of the amphitheatre, the doors of the houses open towards the square through several archways. Although everything but its shape has changed over time, the square still has exceptional acoustics, while the space itself offers a feeling of protection and intimacy.

Bergamo, Italy
Piazza Vechia, Piazza Duomo

Piazza Vecchia was built in the 13th century, when Bergamo was an independent city. It was subsequently extended by the Visconti family, and acquired its final form during the period of Venetian rule, when its red brick and white stone pavements were added. Although the square is beautiful, at first glance it is nothing special compared to other Italian squares: it features a tower, a fountain, a monumental staircase, palaces. What makes this space unique is the passage towards the neighbouring square of the dome, which is smaller and unnoticeable from the Piazza Vecchia, where only the cupolas are visible. The passage is not a narrow street, as in other cities such as San Gimignano or Verona, but an arch at the base of the Palazzo della Ragione, making the act of entering this square a pleasant discovery for those unfamiliar with the city's topography.

Orvieto, Italy
Piazza del Duomo

The dome's square in Orvieto is the typical parvis square of medieval Cathedrals. Paradoxically, these squares that appear everywhere in Europe are not usually large enough to allow a full view of the Cathedral. Orvieto is not an exception, but here the effect is unique. Firstly, the location of the town is spectacular, seated as it is on a very steep volcanic plateau. The Cathedral, built to celebrate the miracle of Bolsena in 1263, stands at the town's highest point, on the site of an Etruscan temple, with the most beautifully decorated façade in the whole of Italy. Orvieto's square is dominated not by the Cathedral, but by its façade, leading to an interesting play between its two-dimensional surface and the three-dimensional plan of the square. The chromatics of the façade create a stark contrast with the gray sobriety of the square. Between the Cathedral and the square, a stretch of decorated pavement ensures the chromatic transition.

Assisi, Italy
Piazza del Comune

Assisi, famous due to Saint Francis, is, through its positioning, yet another exception to the rule of Etruscan settlements. It lies not on a hill, but on a steep side of Mount Subasio. It also holds its own 'secrets'. For one, its shape, irregular like any medieval square, represents the shape of the town in miniature – a coincidence, yet a profoundly symbolic one in the town of Saint Francis. Then, it has a special continuity, for it stands on the site of a Roman cistern. The temple of Minerva also dates from the Roman period, converted into a church in 1539 and admired for its proportions by architects and by Goethe as well. Although not planned this way, the buildings are all nearly the same height, which produces a sensation of unity. There is a single exception, the medieval tower next to the temple of Minerva, which makes the square visible from any corner of the town.

Marostica, Italy
Piazza Castello

Every other year, in the second week of September, the small northern Italian town of Marostica, known as Maròstega in the local Venetian dialect, hosts a game of chess. But in this game, living people play the roles of the wooden figurines, and the square of this tiny medieval town serves as the chessboard, with its pavement designed especially for this purpose. For this reason, the Marostica Piazza Castello is also called the Piazza degli Scacchi ['Chess Square']. A legend tells of two young nobles, Rinaldo D'Angarano and Vieri da Vallanora, who fell madly in love with Lionora, the daughter of a local lord. The custom of the time required that the girl's fate be decided through a duel. But as her father did not wish to make enemies, and wanted no blood spilt, he forbade the duel and proposed a chess game in its stead. The winner would become the husband of the coveted Lionora. The loser would not lose entirely, but instead gain the hand of his younger daughter, Oldrada.

This story has no basis in historical fact: these nobles did not exist, and such a chess match never took place in medieval Marostica. A Dalmatian writer and architect named Mario Mirko Vucetich invented story, just after the Second World War. And the local chess club found it apt to organize a human-sized chess competition every other year, in this scenic medieval square.

Udine, Italy
Piazza della Libertà

Piazza della Libertà is the oldest square in Udine, and is considered the finest square in the Venetian style in *terraferma*, as Venetian continental possessions were called. It was born as an intersection between the main roads at the base of a hill beneath the castle. At the square's edge, one of the roads passes through an archway designed by Palladio. The scenography of the square is spectacular: the colonnade of the Palazzo del Comune is mirrored by that of the Loggia di San Giovanni, on the opposite side. A terrace with statues, columns, and a Renaissance fountain offer spatial dynamism. The line of the square is closed by the clock tower with the castle high in the backdrop. The entire composition can be seen from various angles through the columns of the square's buildings.

Palmanova, Italy
Piazza Grande

Palmanova was built in 1593 as a military town, a star fort for the defense of Venice. The town knew fighting only once in its history, when Venice fought in the Grandisca War against Austria. Its structure, developed by Scamozzi, has remained unchanged to this day.

Although its basic shape is a polygon with nine sides, its central square has six sides, each one directly linked to the entries of the fort. The square could be isolated and defended by barricading the six arteries leading into it. However, this never proved necessary.

Trieste, Italy
Piazza dell'Unità d'Italia

Piazza Grande or Piazza dell'Unità d'Italia is the largest square with a view to the sea in Europe, measuring almost 17000 square meters. Although separated by a road and a promenade, the square and the waters of the Adriatic seem to blend together when seen from the other side of the square, where lies the *Fontana dei Quattro Continenti*, the point where nearly all the important roads of the city lead. Only two flag masts frame the perspective.

The history of the square began in 1252, with the building of the first Palazzo Comunale, but its current look is much newer, reflecting the changes in the second half of the 19th century, when the city was part of the Austro – Hungarian Empire. Most of the monumental buildings that define the square's perimeter were built after 1858.

The lives of European squares vary from city to city, country to country, culture to culture. It is nearly midnight; while a lone traveler might be hurrying home across an empty square in northern Germany, the squares in the Iberian Peninsula are just waking up, as people emerge to eat, drink, and catch each other up on their days. In winter the contrast is not as sharp, as bustling Christmas fairs enliven the northern squares, while the south slows down somewhat. The squares of all European cities pass from season to season through various rhythms and rituals, showing their many faces. But squares can be divided into even more complex categories than northern and southern. Positioned on a map, it can be seen that the squares with a richer historic and aesthetic presence tend to be found in specific regions, forming a sort of network. Long before the Internet, cities were tied to one another through invisible connections, creating somewhat similar urban 'networks'.

Italy is by definition the land of squares. Many squares regarded as masterpieces are found north of Rome. Northern Italy boasts a higher number of squares per city, at times ingeniously interconnected. The South might have relatively fewer squares, but they are no less noteworthy. While it is difficult to find an unknown square in Italy, I have included here a few lesser-known squares of interest to the history of urbanism, such as Palmanova, or the narrow square in the tiny medieval settlement of Pitigliano.

Across the Adriatic, the squares of the Dalmatian Coast have been severely overlooked. Once under the rule of the Republic of Venice (though some settlements date back even further), foreign encounters, particularly with southern Slavic cultures, have left their mark on the local squares. Cities throughout Slovenia, Croatia and Montenegro host such squares, but one finds fascinating squares all throughout the Balkans.

The historic squares of Central Europe, north of the Alps and throughout the former Austro-Hungarian Empire, are a few centuries younger than their Italian counterparts. While visibly influenced by their predecessors, the unique characteristics of the central European squares are not obscured. It may seem surprising that most of these squares are found outside the powerful centre of Austria, but German colonists, deployed by Austro-Hungary, arriving in the early Middle Ages established many of these settlements. The Czech government has recognised more than forty historical cities in Bohemia and Moravia as urban heritage reservations– cities that developed around large, beautiful squares. Although fewer in number, squares throughout Slovakia, Slovenia, Hungary, and Romania follow the same template. Paradoxically, the central European squares are less 'sophisticated' than those in Germany proper, as can be seen by comparing them with some medieval squares that have survived the Second World War bombings, including ones in the Harz Mountains, among others.

Another area containing special squares is the aforementioned Iberian Peninsula. Spain and Portugal are both countries with 'dynamic' squares. Each Spanish settlement, no matter how small, has a Plaza Mayor, which, quite late in the evening, becomes alive and remains alive until deep into the night: a community and family life that can be glimpsed in the rest of Europe through old photos.

Even when squares are 'cultural imports' as recent as the 19th and 20th centuries – such as those in Balkan cities or in the Caucasian countries between the Black Sea and the Caspian Sea – they demonstrate an interesting synthesis of local traditions and histories. Tbilisi, the capital of Georgia, an ancient rest stop for caravans travelling along the Silk Road, has the Meidan square or Vahtang Gorgasali, originally a bazaar on the trade route.

Venice, Italy
Piazza San Marco

San Marco Square lies at the edge of the largest and lowest island in the Venetian lagoon and is the only square in the city called a *piazza*, with all the others called *campo*. It has two distinct zones, yet their function may not be understood without considering the whole, which actually makes them inseparable: the square itself and the San Marco Plaza, which connects to the sea through the molo, the pier. Piazzeta dei Leoncini, with a side marked by the northern wall of the Basilica, opposite the San Marco square, functioned (and still does) as a continuation of the square itself, and thus has an obscured identity. It received its name quite late, after statues of lions, sculpted from red Cottanello marble, were brought into its centre in 1722. Piazzetta San Marco roughly marks the original nucleus of this square, initially planned as a square and courtyard of the Doge's Palace at a time when only a palace chapel existed where the current Basilica is located. The space of the square itself appeared only after the 1156 clogging of a river which cut the actual perimeter in two, and the square became a Square only after Venice underwent a number of historical changes, a communal psychological transformation. Today it is probably the most photographed square in the world, with over twelve million tourists every year.

Piran, Slovenia
Tartinijev trg

Giuseppe Tartini, author of the well-known *Il trillo del Diavolo*, was born in Piran, then called Pirano, part of the Republic of Venice. The Piran square bears his name, as the birthplace of the composer lies on one side of the square. At the time of his birth, however, the place looked completely different. Rather than a square, this area was first a loading dock for fishing boats coming in from the Adriatic, found outside the citadel walls. In time, palaces and grandiose administrative buildings were built closer to the piers. By 1894, the importance of the area grew enough that the authorities decided to silt the gulf and build a true square. Two years later, Tartini's statue was unveiled, seen as a focal point, and the square, dominated from the hill by the Saint George church and with a campanile identical to the one in Venice, became a harmonious and lively space, with a proper and accomplished balance of form and proportion.

Ljubljana, Slovenia
Prešernov trg, Mestni trg

Prešernov trg was a simple crossroads at the entrance to the medieval city, where, in 1646, a Franciscan monastery was built and remains to this day. In the 19th century, the crossroads was paved and began to resemble an urban square. The end of the same century brought about a radical transformation, as an earthquake in 1895 resulted in the old houses being replaced by Neoclassical and, later, Sezession style buildings. In 1980, the Slovenian architect Edvard Ravnikar created the current circular design of its pavement, which lends a special note to this square: a sun, on a granite background, with rays made of Macedonian Prilep marble. A triple bridge, Tromostovje, across the Ljubljanica, ties the square through Stritarjeva ulica to the old square, found at the foot of the hill where the castle and cathedral are situated. The city square, Mestni trg, is dominated by a fountain built in 1751. The two squares, though not planned together, as each was partly the result of later redevelopments, represent an unexpectedly coherent and suggestive urban whole.

Rovinj, Croatia
Trg Svete Eufemije, Trg G. Matteottija

The history of this city is tied to Venice, but Rovinj was built much earlier, at the start of the 8th century, on an island separated from land by a narrow canal. Much later, in 1763, towards the end of Venetian rule, the community silted the isthmus and the city was united with the mainland. Through a classic process of *synoecism*, a new system of squares formed precisely on the site of the old canal. Numbering four in total, the most important is Trg G. Matteottija. Most of the buildings here are from the 19th century, but they celebrate the city's previous links with Venice, even recreating the lion of San Marco on the city hall's pediment. The main square of the city remains Trg Svete Eufemije, found at the highest point on the hill. Unobstructed on three sides, it gazes out to the sea, dominated by the 60-meter campanile of the basilica, with a statue of Saint Euphemia at the top, rotating in the breeze.

Split, Croatia
Trg Peristil

From a bird's eye view, the old town of Split resembles a rectangular box filled with buildings, streets and markets. Beginning in the Middle Ages, two of the larger markets in the citadel played a key role in the history of the city, Narodni Trg, or Spalato in Italian. The People's Square, called simply *Pjaca* by the locals, was first mentioned in the 13th century, and features a number of superb Gothic buildings. A bit further on, at the entrance to the citadel, lies Trg Braće Radić, called Voćni Trg by the locals, meaning 'fruit market,' in reference to its earlier, colourful identity. Just outside the medieval walls is a third great square, Republic Square. Its more recent architecture reminds one of Venice's San Marco. It was built in the mid-19th century, in a historicist style, demonstrating that Split, long under Venetian rule, still carries on this tradition.

But the oldest and most interesting of the Split squares is the smaller Trg Peristril, considered the historical heart of the area by locals. Originally the interior courtyard of a palace built for the Roman emperor Diocletian in 305, measuring 300 square meters, it is the best-preserved Roman palace to this day. In fact, half of the old city of Split lies within the palace walls. After the Romans abandoned it, it remained uninhabited for centuries, until the people of Salona took refuge there from the invading Slavs, turning the former palace into their settlement. And a settlement it shall remain. When John of Ravenna, first archbishop of the region, oversaw the transformation of the Diocletian mausoleum into a church the palace courtyard officially became known as Cathedral Square.

Dubrovnik, Croatia
Trg Luža, Gundulićeva poljana

Trg Luža, the large square in Dubrovnik, lies at the end of the largest artery crossing the citadel from west to east, called Stradun or Placa. Each extremity represents a point of entry into the citadel, marked by a gate and a square. This structure, clearly visible in an aerial photograph, is linked to the way the city was once built. Ten centuries ago, Stradun's current path was a canal separating the old Greco-Roman colony Ragusa, which was established on an island, from Dubrva, the settlement of the continental Slavs. In the 11th century, the canal was silted and the two communities became one, although their rivalry and mutual contempt would never disappear. A century later, they were still located within the same walls. In accordance with the classic plan of the process of *synoecism*, the main square was shaped at the geographical contact point between the two communities. Thus, Trg Luža was born, which would also contain the most important historical buildings: Orlando's statue, the Palace of the Rector, the Sponza Palace, the Clock Tower, Onufri's small well. The well's street unites Luža square with the second most important market, Gundulićeva Poljana, which was built much later, after the earthquake of 1667. Although planned separately, the two squares comprise an integrated system.

Zadar, Croatia
Trg Rimskog Foruma

The urban structure of present-day Zadar dates back to the time of Julius Caesar. A Roman municipium, called Iader, was built here soon after the province of Illyricum was established in 59 BC. As unlikely as it would seem, its regular structure is perfectly visible in the structure of the current town, despite the passing of years and the continuous inhabitations that could have modified it. The square is actually the Roman *forum* itself, the largest on the eastern shore of the Adriatic, and features some columns and bits of original pavement.

Motovun, Croatia
Trg Andrea Antico

The Andrea Antico square in Motovun is the only flat place in this tiny hill-town. The Etruscans were not the only ones to build hill-towns; they are also quite numerous in the Istrian peninsula, present-day Croatia. Motovun, or Montona in Italian, is the most beautiful

of all such towns, with its narrow streets and efficient use of limited space. Its double fortifications and urban structure date from the Venetian period. This small square appears much larger than it actually is, in comparison with the rest of the town.

Trogir, Croatia
Trg Ivana Pavla II

Trogir was founded as a Greek colony in the 3rd century BC, and expanded significantly during the Roman period. In 1412, Trogir, or Trau, as it was then called, belonged to Venice, and remained in its possession for four hundred years. In short, this town encompasses over 2300 years of continuous urban tradition. Its orthogonal structure, containing Romanic and Gothic churches, as well as Renaissance and Baroque-style palaces, stems from the Hellenistic period. The square stands on the exact site of a Roman *forum*, perhaps even that of a Greek agora, and the Cathedral stands on the site of a temple dedicated to Hera.

Poreč, Croatia
Trg Marafor, Trg Slobode

Trg Marafor, the largest square in Poreč (or Parenzo, in Italian), lies at the sea-end of a peninsula, with its name stemming from the words Mars and *forum*. Poreč was the site of an important Roman *castrum*. The *forum* held a temple to the god Mars, the greatest Roman temple on the eastern Adriatic. Several of its columns survive to this day. The square also preserves parts of its original 1st century pavement. The busiest street in the town is called Decumanus. In the Roman city-building system, *decumanus* was the name for arteries oriented on an east-west axis, with the *decumanus maximus* signifying the main artery of this type. The *forum* was built close to where it intersected with the main north-south artery, called the *cardo maximus*. Between the *cardo maximus* and the *decumanus maximus*, the *cardo* usually held the primary role. But sometimes, for geographical reasons, this hierarchy was reversed. This is precisely what happened in Poreč. The walled medieval town built its streets over those of the Roman *castrum*, copying their regular structure. On the other end of the peninsula one finds Trg Slobode, or Liberty Square, which is smaller and newer, but now serves as Poreč's main square, as well as a meeting place for the Italian community, which maintains a strong presence in the town.

Šibenik, Croatia
Trg Republike Hrvatske

Šibenik is an exception among the towns on the Dalmatian coast. It did not originate as a Greek colony, nor was it founded by Illyrians or Romans, but by the first Croats to settle here. Yet its later history was not so different from that of other coastal towns, impacted by the arrival of the Ottomans, the Venetians, the Kings of Hungary and the Habsburgs. But the Slavs always remain the dominant element in the citadel. For a time, the Istro-Romanian community was numerous here.

The square has distinct nuances and is considered the most beautiful in present-day Croatia. It contains two sections, one of which was the church square, whereas the other was the centre of secular power; although close to the shore, it was never a port. The important landmarks of the square are its Renaissance-style palace, and the Church of St. Jacob, which is part of the UNESCO list.

Kotor, Montenegro

Trg od Oružja, Trg od Brašna, Pjaca Svetog Tripuna, Trg Sveti Luke

Kotor, or Cattaro in Italian, owes its fortifications and urban structure to the Venetian period – as do many other cities along the Dalmatian coast – although this settlement has had various masters over time. Independent in the early Middle Ages, it became part of the Bulgarian Tsardom, then part of Stefan Nemanja's Great Principality of Serbia, and then part of the Kingdom of Hungary. When it was threatened and temporarily conquered by the Ottomans, it sought the protection of Venice. When Venice itself fell, the Napoleonic armies entered the region, followed by the Austrian-Hungarian Empire. Kotor became part of Yugoslavia after the First World War. For such a small place, its large number of squares is astounding. The city is akin to a labyrinth of narrow streets and unexpectedly wide squares. No fewer than four of these serve as main squares. Two of them have Slavic names (Trg od Oružja, Trg od Brašna); and one bears the ancient title of 'square' (Piaca Svetog Tripuna). The fourth has several names, pointing equally to its Slavic and Venetian roots (Trg Sveti Luke/ Piazza Greca). The very interesting Saint Luca church stands here. Built in 1195, this was originally a Roman-Catholic church, but since 1657 it has featured two altars, Catholic and Orthodox, side by side.

Herceg Novi, Montenegro
Trg Herceg Stjepana

Herceg Novi, or Castelnuovo in Italian, is not as new as its name claims, but rather quite old, founded in 1382 on the site of a fishing village by the Bosnian King Stephen I, which is also the name of this town's central square. The Turks conquered the town in 1482 and remained there for two centuries, with a brief Spanish interlude.

The town came under Venetian rule in 1687, and then passed to Austro-Hungary. After that, Herceg Novi was temporarily ruled by Napoleon, the Russians and Mussolini, and then became part of Yugoslavia. Its history, though not in its entirety, can be found in its square. It is a paradoxical square, built in a typically Italian style, with a splendid Orthodox church in the middle, surrounded by palm trees. Unofficially, the name of the square is Belavista. From there the sea is visible, as well as an Ottoman clock tower, a Spanish fortress, the bell tower of the Catholic church and the lower part of the city.

Perast, Montenegro
Trg Sveti Nikole

This urban structure dates from the time of the town's greatest economic growth, under Venetian rule. As in many coastal towns, the square is also a port. Here one finds the city hall to the west and the livestock market to the east. On the northern side, the church of St. Nicholas has the highest bell tower on the Adriatic coast. A so-called 'balota' stone marks the place where the port-square ends and where the church square begins, indicating that the way the space was structured was very important for the community.

Kruševo,
Republic of North Macedonia
Cearshia

Kruševo, or Crușova in Aromanian, is the tallest town in the entire Balkan Peninsula, located on Bushova mountain. The architecture is interesting and atypical, midway between Europe and the East. The town was built by wealthy Aromanians, forced to migrate after Moscopole was burnt down by the Ottomans, along with Slavs from the Mijak group, who were very skilled in house-building. The central square brings together different traditions. Kruševo, like all towns influenced by Turkish traditions in the Balkans, was not planned and had not square. But the Aromanian trade with Europe led to the need for the organization of the space in the 19th century, thus bringing about a diffuse square. Its history can be understood only in contrast to the intricate map of the surrounding streets. Its name comes from a Turkish word, meaning „centre", and refers to the entirety of the town's middle, not only to the square itself.

The etymologies of the words for squares in languages spoken across Europe each have an interesting story to tell.

The Greek term Πλατεῖα, meaning 'square', comes from the joining of two terms, Πλατεῖα Ὁδὸς (*plateia odos*), meaning 'wide road'. Thus, the word 'wide' came to refer to the square. In Latin Πλατεῖα became *platea*. *Plaza* in Spanish, *piazza* in Italian, *praça* in Portuguese, *place* in French, *piața* in Romanian, *place* in English, *Platz* in German – all come directly or through an intermediary language from the Latin word.

The Polish and Czech word *rynek* derives from Middle High German *rinc*, 'town square', originally *ring*, or 'circle'. This is an interesting inversion of meaning because the idea of the circle refers to the edges of the city, once marked by walls, and not to the center. The Czech term *náměstí* and the Slovak word *námestie* both mean 'in the town' (*město/ mesto* is 'town'). *Trg* comes from the Proto-Slavic word тъrgъ, 'town', of uncertain origin, and *ploshchead* from a Proto-Slavic word meaning 'flat'.

Many of the countries towards the east of Europe that came into contact with the Ottoman Empire use the term *meidan*. Taksim Meydanı is the main square in the European part of Istanbul, while the main square in the historical area is Sultan Ahmed Meydanı. The central square of Kiev, which captured the world's attention during the 2014 demonstrations, is called Maidan. In Ukrainian, the word arrives from Turkish through the Crimean Tatars. Tavisuplebis Moedani is the central market in Tbilisi, Georgia. Tatar, Tajik, Bashkir, Azerbaijani, Uzbek, Uighur languages all retain inflections of the word *maidan* to mean square. The word can be found, with exactly the same meaning, in a number of languages throughout Eastern Europe, including Georgian, Russian, Ukrainian and Armenian, with archaic variants also existing in Czech and Serbo-Croatian.

The word *meidan* possesses an entire cultural history. In Turkish, the term comes from Persian. Maidān-e Naqsh-e Jahān, built between 1528 and 1629, is the massive square in Isfahan. Measuring 160 meters by 508 meters, it far exceeds Jan Gehl's 100 meter limit for interactions to take place at a human scale. Impressed by its grandeur, Pietro Della Valle, an Italian traveller of the 17th century, proclaimed that its beauty surpassed that of Piazza Navona in his native Rome. The Maidan in Isfahan draws inspiration from the famed Persian gardens rather than the European square, which is why, for instance, *maidan* also means 'park' in the Indian cultural space – for example, the central park in Calcutta is named Maidan. The squares called *maidan* – through etymologically related words – represent an overlapping of eastern traditions and mentalities with the European square. It is likely that the impressive square in Isfahan is responsible for *maidan* becoming equivalent to 'square'. In Persian, *maidan* also means 'square', but the word comes from Arabic, where it simply means 'city'. Medina is thus the city par excellence. The Persians inherited *maidan* from Pahlavi, Median Persian, where *mēd* meant 'middle'. *Maidan* is also found in Sanskrit as *madhya*, and linguists have reconstructed the Indo-European root *$méd^hyos$, whose reflex is also the Latin word medius, or 'middle', as in the supposed etymon, the middle of the world.

How did the 'middle' turn into 'city'? Consider that in all the old worlds, the space of one's own life was situated in the middle of the world. Present in so many languages and cultures – meaning 'city', 'square-garden' in Persian, then only 'square' or 'park' in India – the word changed little in meaning. The essential component of the square remains conceptually as the middle of the inhabited world.

Istanbul, Turkey
Sultanahmet Meydanı

This square bears some of the ambiguities of the meeting point between the Orient and Europe. This is not a single square, but rather two squares brought together and identically named. Between the Hagia Sophia and Sultan Ahmet Camii, known as the Blue Mosque, lies a square with a fountain at its centre, often called Ayasofya Meydani, although the official name is Sultanahmet Meydani. This is a market-garden, built on the spot which held the Roman *forum* of Augustus. Paradoxically, the long square between the Blue Mosque and the Museum of Islamic Art has kept the name Sultanahmet Park, although it is less of a park than the neighbouring square. There is no place in the world that brings together so much history. The obelisk of Theodosius the Great is, in fact, Egyptian, and was brought here in 390, from Luxor. Sculpted in Aswan granite, it was built in 1490 B.C. for the Egyptian pharaoh Thutmose III. The serpentine column was brought in 324 to the temple of Apollo at Delphi, where it marked the victory of the Greeks against the Persians. Cast from the alloy of the Persian weapons and melted down by the Greeks, it is now 2500 years old. Another obelisk was built in the 10th century by Constantin VII. One must also add the 'German fountain' built in 1900 to mark the visit of Kaiser Wilhelm II. The Blue Mosque and the Hagia Sophia define one side of the square; on the opposite side, the Museum of Islamic Art is found in the palace of Ibrahim Pasha, the vizier of Suleyman the Magnificent. A marble column marks the kilometer zero of the Eastern Roman Empire, still visible in the northeastern corner of the square. And this is not all: the square is, in fact, the arena of the Roman hippodrome.

Tbilisi, Georgia
Meidan Bazaar

This urban square was an important trading node, where the caravans of the long Silk Road could meet and exchange wares. In the 18th century, Meidan was mentioned on Vaxushti Batonisvhili's map as Citadel's Square. As he was passing through the Caucasus to Persia after the middle of the 18th century, Jean Chardin, a French jeweler and traveller, wrote: 'nowhere in the world will you see a greater mix of peoples from all the corners of the earth: Armenians, Greeks, Jews, Persians, Tatars, Muscovites and Europeans of all sorts…' In short, one could say that this square was the greatest livestock market of the Caucasus. Today it is officially called Vakhtang Gorgasali Square, but everyone knows it as Meidan.

Tbilisi, Georgia
Tavisuplebis Moedani

A true symbol of Georgian independence, this area was named Freedom Square in 1918, during the First Georgian Republic. The name returned after the collapse of the USSR, proudly defining the country's current identity, strengthened by the golden statue of Saint George defeating the dragon, which was placed here in 2006. It is interesting to note how the successive names of the square perfectly represent the history of Georgia in the modern age. When the square was built at the beginning of the 19th century, it was called Erevan or Ivan Paskevich Square – named after the general of the Russian Imperial Army, who conquered Erevan, eventually receiving the title of Count of Erevan. During the time of the USSR it was first called Beria Square, then Lenin Square, with a statue of Lenin dominating the centre until 1991.

An interesting glimpse into the dynamics of the urban network of the city: at first, when this area was an intersection of trading routes with an inn, rather than a square, it was located towards the margins of the settlement. The gradual development of the commercial outlying area of the city eventually became a centre, something encountered in many large Western European cities. A noteworthy historic episode took place here in 1907, when the square was witness to a famous bank heist organised and led by Stalin himself.

Sarajevo, Bosnia and Herzegovina
Baščaršija

Baščaršija dates back to the 15th century, when İshakoğlu İsa Bey, the Turkish governor of Bosnia, built Sarajevo. In keeping with the Oriental urban tradition, the cities have no square but a bazaar – this is what Baščaršija means and it was the commercial, administrative and cultural heart of the place. Here, mosques were built, along with shops, a library, a clock tower and inns. When the city became part of Austro-Hungary in 1878, the new rulers desired its transformation into a European city. A fire aided the architects' plans and the central space of the bazaar, dominated by a minaret built in the 16th century, became a square. Today, it is unofficially known as 'Dove square'.

Thessaloniki, Greece
Plateia Aristotelous

The history of Aristotelous square began with a fire that destroyed two thirds of the city in 1917. Until then– due to centuries of Ottoman rule – Thessaloniki was an Oriental city, with no square. Moreover, any attempt to design one had been thwarted by the impossibility of demolishing an area which had been built too densely. However, that which cannot be achieved by architects can be accomplished by fire. The project was prepared by Frenchman Ernest Hébrard in 1918, but finalised only in 1950.

Kallarites, Greece
Plateia

At more than 1200 meters in altitude, Kalarites, called Călarli in the local Aromanian-Vlach idiom, is perched on a nearly barren plateau, above a deep ravine with walls 500 meters high. This ravine forms part of the valley through which the Kalariticos River flows and which, in contrast to the barrenness of the region where the village is situated, is dominated by rich vegetation. It is not precisely known when the history of this place began. The presence of the Aromanians in the region is mentioned in Byzantine documents from the 10th century. Around 1750, Kalarites became an important trading centre, renowned for its silver and gold work, and it underwent a period of great development until 1821. This square is set on a slope, with its northern side consisting of the stone steps of an amphitheatre, at one end of which stands a parish house, built in 1869. At the edge of the steps stands an ancient tree, strangely positioned. Immediately behind, to one side of the square, stands the café of Napoleon Zagalis. Narrow stairs and a system of stone mini-terraces contribute to the picturesque atmosphere of the square's corner. The house of the priest, the former school, a shop and a café all complete the setting.

Syrrako, Greece
Plateia

This square lies at the southern extremity of the settlement and on its lowest side, just above a steep valley. A ring of houses, set in concentric semicircles to the north, create an amphitheatre above it. The square is built on two levels. The first is represented by the courtyard of the church of Saint Nicholas. Dating from the 15th century, this is the main church of the community. The connection to the lower level is made through a road parallel to the two levels. Here one finds two impressively thick ancient trees. Syrrako, called Sereacu in the local Aromanian idiom, is first mentioned in historical records from the 15th century, but locals are certain it was inhabited much earlier. The main argument they offer is the age of the trees, planted at the founding of the settlement by the Aromanians. On one side is a café. Towards the valley, there is an old store, but it is situated somewhat lower than the level of the square, so that the southern side offers a large opening towards the road leading to the settlement, the precipice and the mountain top.

Vovousa, Greece
Plateia

Vouvousa, called Băiasa in Aromanian, is one of the most well-known Aromanian villages in Greece, the eastern most settlement of Zagori.

Right in the middle of the village one finds the square, divided into three terraces, bordered by the road and the Aoos river, called Băiasa by the Aromanians. At the centre of the square is a tree that someday will become ancient. The project of this square is new and was planned by the Romanian architect Vasile Marcu. Next to the old and beautiful upper level church there is another, much older square, which has two terraces. The first is the church courtyard, with its stone fountain. The second section of the square has a triangular shape, with a tree in the middle, planted in 1768, that boasts the grandeur of centuries past. All around it, very close to the trunk, along a specially built stone terrace, are benches facing the tree rather than the square. An interesting way to imagine a conversation!

The photos in this book have been the subject of exhibitions that have traveled to over twenty cities in eleven different countries – Romania, Spain, Turkey, Italy, Bulgaria, Greece, Poland, Georgia, Azerbaijan, Portugal and Ireland. In August 2018, a special presentation of this exhibition took place as an experiment in visual anthropology, when the images travelled to the Aromanian settlements of the Pindus Mountains of Greece. These isolated villages are not well-known, and are rarely visited by tourists. The inhabitants are speakers of a neo-Latin language, Aromanian, predominantly oral and now on the verge of extinction – with few exceptions, the younger generations do not speak it. The exhibition was set up without prior notice, but with the permission of local authorities. The event was organised precisely in the main squares of these old stone settlements, with locals surprised to find images of their own squares alongside other, better-known squares.

The anthropologist Cătălin D. Constantin, author of the exhibition, has conducted extensive fieldwork in the area, returning often in recent years. He has written on the subject more broadly in his book, European Squares and their Histories. He has come to know many inhabitants, some of which are now close friends, from the settlements where the exhibition took place. The settlements, Călarli

and Seracu, are called Kalarites and Syrako in Greek. The unique way of life in Kalarites and Syrako is a result of the now-declining pastoral lifestyle. In the summer, the villages are brimming with energy as the population rises into the hundreds, even thousands. In the winter, however, snow closes off most of the roads, ensuring that at most six or seven people remain. As a result, the community has traditionally functioned according to norms that differ from those of permanently settled communities. The social activities and events that revolve around the settlements' squares during the summer, when the community regroups, help maintain social ties. The very birth of every Aromanian settlement in these mountains is linked to the centuries-old plane trees that crown these squares.

Traditionally, before founding a settlement, the Aromanians would pray for a sign that the site was protected and suitable for living. They would plant a tree, usually a plane tree, and, if it prospered for a number of years, they would take this as a sign of a good place to settle. A square would be built around this tree; Then came the houses. The square with the tree at its heart symbolically unified the community, because the time spent in the square – either in rituals or day-to-day activities – stabilised and strengthened the community, whose members were otherwise dispersed throughout the rest of the year.

Field Journal Excerpts

Cota's mule is the only method of transporting materials into the village square, where I installed the exhibition, under the astonished gaze of villagers seated at the local café, having just returned from the church service. I chose Sunday for this very reason. Then other visitors appeared. In less than two hours, the whole village had come to witness the first exhibition to ever take place in the square. Tanase is a craftsman who builds and restores the unique stone-shingled rooftops in the area. I have known him since the winter of 2014. Cota's brothers and sisters were of course also there along with Anastasios from Syrrako, Napoleon… even a few tourists. Vasilis constantly took pictures. I've known him for two days now. 'You are an interesting man and I would like to buy you a coffee', he said, before he knew about the exhibition or who I was, suddenly stopping me in a stone alley on my very first morning in Călarli. Something made him understand that, although I was a foreigner, I somehow also belonged. He's retired, has travelled a

lot and used to work as an economist. He is well-off and lives in Athens. He wasn't born in the village; he first came to Călarli when he was 14, visiting his grandparents. It was then that he learned Aromanian and fell in love with the place. He comes only once a year, for communion at the local church. But it is also, he says, because Călarli is the only place in Greece where you can see seven mountains at once while you drink your coffee at the tavern by the entrance to the village.

§

One of the shepherds stood by for half an hour, watching the drone photograph the village. Eventually he called me over and said simply that the photo was not framed properly – I should set it horizontally, not vertically, in contrast to the others, so that his houses (he has several, side by side) would appear straight. Then he began, also in Aromanian, to talk about everything that could be seen from above. Then he asked for detailed explanations about the other images on display. In a short time, he had become a guide and curator, able to explain anything to any visitor. I was no longer needed. His

son is the owner of the square's café, a pleasant young man. We talk, in a way – he only speaks Greek. He took pictures of the exhibition with his mobile phone and uploaded them to the café's Facebook page, where it was widely distributed among the Facebook groups of the Greek Vlachs.

§

A brother and sister, two cheerful children, around 5 years old. I had the feeling they were the children of Tanase's brother. Suddenly the boy approached me and determinedly took my camera. He could barely hold it, as it weighs several kilos. He sent his sister to the row of photos on display with a cheerful command. His sister, a year or two younger, positioned herself with the self-assurance of a professional model. She really knew how to pose. He asked her to come towards him with a running step. They tried several different shots and angles. They spoke to me in Greek, reacted as if I understood everything perfectly, and didn't care that I answered in another language. The dialogue went on like this for a quarter of an hour in a very natural way. This resulted in a series of photos taken by the boy with a certain degree of confidence. A few of them were taken absolutely correctly. I had to help him with the camera – it weighed him down – but he wouldn't give up. Instead, he knew exactly which button to press and how to direct the lens. He had probably been watching me carefully beforehand, without my realising it. The observed observer. The researched researcher.

§

The 'delegation' of nephews from the neighbouring village of Syrrako/Seracu arrived in the afternoon in Kallarites/Călarli, in order to see the exhibition. Their journey was made on foot and took about two hours. A deep and narrow valley divides these two nearby villages. In brief, the nephews told me that yesterday they had won a football match against Matzuki, another neighbouring village; that they have

Romanian Carpathian sheepherding dogs; that their village is more beautiful than the village where the exhibition was held; that the landscapes here are more beautiful than in Romania, though Romanian girls are more beautiful than their own; and that in these villages they speak 'the same language as in your country.' All of this was relayed to me in English, and a very good one at that. They never learned Aromanian, but they shared their stories with such enthusiasm! Among them were the nephews of Barba Lefterie, an 81-year-old Aromanian from Syrako, who gifted me with my first ever shepherd's crook. He is very dear to me, and visited me two years ago in Bucharest. The night ended in the square of the neighbouring village, that is, Syrako, for Barba Lefterie called us in the evening to say that he was expecting us for the Agia Sotiria party. He wanted to see us and, of course, to show hospitality since my cousin Carmen had paid for his nephews' meal that afternoon in Călarli square.

§

I wanted to see the reactions of a small community, an isolated settlement, to these photographs. That is, to see locals' perceptions of their own settlement, photographed from a perspective they had never seen before but could link to other squares and well-known places. In anthropological theory, one speaks of the need to 'return home' – to give back to the community that has been studied – the information gathered by the anthropologist after completing a publication. This is what I did in Kalarites, albeit in visual form. The book was leafed through and requested, of course, for its images. It was here that I had the most offers to buy the images in the exhibition, and all were disappointed when I said they were not for sale as I only had a single copy of each one. In the end, I gave the photograph with the drone's view of the settlement to Napoleon, for his café, the first place I had stopped when I reached Călarli with Dan, that first winter.

Sofia, Bulgaria
Ploshcead Sveti Aleksandar Nevski

Immediately after 1878, when Bulgaria gained its independence, plans began for an imposing cathedral to be built in Sofia. The foundation stone was placed in 1882. The cathedral was dedicated to Saint Alexander Nevsky, in memory of the Russian soldiers. Around the cathedral, one of the first modern squares in the Balkans began to take shape. It is a space with great symbolic significance, for it also holds the more modestly sized church of Saint Sofia (4th – 6th centuries), which is delightful in its age and proportions, and which has given the city its name.

Tryavna, Bulgaria
Ploshchead Kapitan Diado Nikola

Founded four centuries ago at the foot of the Balkans, Tryavna was inhabited by carpenters and woodworkers, icon painters and house builders. The development of crafts also meant urban development. Tryavna's square includes buildings in the so-called 'Bulgarian Renaissance' style, which emerged in the 18th and 19th centuries. It features traditional houses with porches and inner courtyards, with rooftops made from stone slabs; a large 13th century church; an arched bridge made of stone. The focal point of the square is its clock tower, built in 1814. This is one of dozens of clock towers

existing in Balkan city squares. A geographical paradox, rather than a cultural one: such towers are expressions of Westernisation, but they come from the east, from Istanbul and Anatolia, where the European ones were first copied. The oldest of such towers in the Ottoman Empire was built in 1798, when none of the Balkan houses likely had clocks, as measuring time was not as important then.

Bucharest, Romania
Piața Universității

This is one of the most important squares in Bucharest, with a shape influenced by Haussmann's model of grand intersections. By the end of the 15th century, this was located at the edge of the city, but today it often plays the role of Bucharest's central square, and, in recent history, it has been the scene of many great public demonstrations. This was the first school of higher studies in Wallachia originally stood, the Saint Sava Academy, upon which the University of Bucharest was later built in the mid-19th century. The square holds five statues of important figures of Romanian history, one of which was recently remade, as it had been destroyed at the beginning of the Communist period.

Brașov, Romania
Piața Sfatului

Already from the 14th century, markets were constantly held in Piața Sfatului in Brașov and produce was exchanged. Back then it was called Marktplatz. Casa Sfatului, constructed in 1420, dominates the space. It not only forms the centre of the square, but also offers an interesting chromatic counterpoint, through its light colour, to the nearby Schwarze Kirche, the Black Church, visible from the square.

Sibiu, Romania
Piața Mare, Piața Mică

Called Großer Ring in German, Piața Mare was first mentioned in the 14th century. It served as a stage for main events but also as a site for public executions. The square contained, in typical central European style, a statue of Roland; a cage for the insane; and a column of St. John Nepomouk, which today stands in the courtyard of the Catholic church. Piața Mică, or the Kleiner Ring, initially lay outside the town's walls, and owes its existence to Sibiu's second fortification. The houses built during that period followed the circular path of the old defense walls, which explains why the buildings in this square have a circular shape. The arches on the ground floor hosted shops belonging to the local guilds.

Alba Iulia, Romania
Piața Cetății

Alba Iulia has the largest Vauban-style fortress in southeastern Europe. It was built between 1716 and 1735 on the site where a medieval citadel and a Roman castrum once stood. Designed by the Italian architect Giovanni Morando Visconti and approved by Eugene of Savoy, the fortress has six triumphal gates and seven bastions. At the exact geometrical centre of the star, it has a large quadrilateral square, typical of Vauban-style fortresses.

Timișoara, Romania

Piața Unirii, Piața Libertății, Piața Victoriei

In 1716, the troops of Eugene of Savoy conquered Timișoara from the Turks. The Austrians decided to build one of the greatest bastion-fortresses in Europe. Its fortifications would be demolished in the 19th century, but the two very beautiful squares, built in the typical Central-European style, have remained. Victoriei Square has its origins in the urban projects of the late 19th century, but it was completed in the 20th century and is the place where the fall of communism began in Romania in 1989.

Tarnów, Poland
Rynek

Rynek, the square in Tarnów, has remained unchanged in shape and size since its beginnings in 1330, when King Władysław Łokietek granted the governor of Krakow the right to establish a city here. Tarnów stood on one of the main trading routes of the continent, which, cutting through Galicia, connected Krakow to Lvov. The square is centrally positioned, on a sloped terrain, which was chosen specifically so the rainwater would drain more easily. Its current buildings are obviously younger than the square itself, as the original wooden ones were destroyed by fires. At the square's centre is a 14th century City Hall building, flanked by a brick tower – originally a defensive structure. The merchant houses, nearly all of them two stories tall, were constructed between the 16th and 18th centuries. Number 20 – built in 1566 and the property of a very wealthy Scottish merchant – especially draws one's attention.

Krakow, Poland
Rynek Główny

Rynek Główny, the Central Square of Krakow, is considered the largest medieval square in Europe. It was built in 1257, during Krakow's reconstruction after it had been destroyed by the Mongolian Invasions of 1241.

The square holds a central position in the carefully planned grid of this medieval trading settlement, where three streets enter the square perpendicularly, each equidistant from one another. Its only irregularity, significant to the structure of the town, is an opening in the shape of a funnel, which leads to a street connected to the hill of the Wawel Castle.

Sukiennice, or the Hall of the Drapers, the longitudinal building at its centre, divides the square into two nearly identical spaces. These, together with the tower of the former City Hall and the Church of Saint Wojciech simultaneously unify the large square, while each 'flaunts' its individuality in an otherwise relatively uniform space. The façade of Saint Mary's church is not positioned on the grid of the city and thus directs one's gaze beyond the square. Rynek Główny is considered one of the finest squares in Europe.

Retz, Austria

Hauptplatz

In 1278, Emperor Rudolph I von Habsburg granted Count Berthold von Rabenswal the right of ownership to the Hardegg land. The count immediately set to work on a new settlement next to an existing village called Rezze. He followed a well-ordered construction plan, in the style of the Bohemian burgs, around a square that remains

among the largest in Austria to this day, although the current population of this settlement numbers only 4000. The square houses Italian-inspired Renaissance palaces, fountains and a Baroque column of the Holy Trinity. At its centre stands the City Hall, a former church that was repurposed in 1569. A greater surprise lies beneath the pavement: under the square, under the entire town and beyond, lies a labyrinth of interconnected cellars, where inhabitants used to store their wines. This underground structure is over twenty kilometers wide, even greater than the network of streets above.

Mikulov, Czech Republic
Náměstí

This square is called simply Náměstí Square. It is very small, but incredibly beautiful. In its current form, it dates from the end of the 16th century. Important elements include: the *sgraffito* house, also called the Knights' House; the column of the Holy Trinity; a fountain from the end of the 18th century depicting Pomona with a Cornucopia in her hands; and a former Baroque church turned into a crypt for the Dietrichstein family.

    A castle, built in the 13th century, dominates the square – its gardens make it resemble a toy model. From the square, one sees a hill with an unusually perfect curve. A pilgrimage chapel dedicated to Saint Sebastian crowns the summit of the hill – called the Holy Hill, which is a destination for pilgrims. The square is set on a slope, and the position of the buildings, as well the views they afford of the surrounding landscape, castle, and tower on the Holy Hill, give it the appearance of a stage set.

Znojmo, Czech Republic

Masarykovo náměstí, Horní náměstí

This town stands on a rock perilously suspended above the Dyje River, in a region with great and ancient viticultural traditions. Documented as early as 1046, Znojmo, or Znaim in German, has two large squares, united by a single narrow street. Connecting the two in the middle stands the tower of the City Hall, built in 1445. The larger square, Masarykovo náměstí, was significantly damaged during the Second World War and is marked by obvious stylistic differences. At its northern end, one finds the concrete building of a socialist supermarket, while a Capuchin monastery stands at the southern end. A few of the surrounding buildings are noteworthy in their Baroque decorations and Gothic details. At the centre stands a typical plague column, with a statue of the Virgin flanked by four saints.

České Budějovice, Czech Republic

Náměstí Přemysla Otakara II

This square is among the largest in Europe, and bears the name of King Ottokar II of Bohemia, who in 1256 founded the town, called Budweis in German. The Black Tower, built in the 16th century, and the Cathedral of Saint Nicholas are located in its south-eastern corner. The Baroque City Hall building lies at the opposite corner, while Samson's Fountain, featuring elaborate Baroque decorations, marks the square's centre. Forty-eight houses with coats of arms, a beer brewery, and a salt market occupy out the rest of the square.

Slavonice, Czech Republic
Náměstí Míru, Horní náměstí

Called Zlabings in German, and first mentioned in 1260, Slavonice lies one kilometre from the Austrian border. Its geographic position might be the reason its architecture has survived to this day. Removing the flourishing town from the trading route uniting Prague to Vienna, kept the Renaissance architecture and the original plan intact. And once again, after expelling the German population in 1945, the town, so close to the frontier, has remained deserted – and spared from the Socialist bulldozer of apartment block building – by the new authorities, In later years, it was renovated and transformed into an artist colony.

The town's plan is atypical, with two interconnected squares. One of them, called Peace Square, is triangular whereas the other, called Upper Square, is elongated and has the church as its central point, surrounded by houses. A large number of buildings from the late Gothic and Renaissance periods are practically intact, with many façades decorated with a special type of *sgraffito*.

Český Krumlov, Czech Republic

Náměstí Svornosti

Náměstí Svornosti is a small square, 45 by 60 meters, grouping together a number of houses with Renaissance façades, a Baroque column, and an old City Hall building with an arched and covered walkway. The town, called Krumau in German, grew around a splendid castle, whose first historical mention dates back to a 13th century poem. The castle has always remained a focal point, whilst the square held a secondary role, which accounts for its size, also determined by its location on a bend of the Vltava River. Nonetheless, it remains a key element of the fairy-tale like atmosphere of the settlement, which has become renowned across the world and, thus, is still visited by many tourists.

Tábor, Czech Republic
Žižkovo náměstí

On one side of this square stands a statue of Jan Žižka, leader of the Hussite movement and one of the few military commanders in history to have never lost a battle. Today, his name is found in this square in Tábor. Situated on a hilltop, with the square at its peak, and near Lake Jordan, named after the Biblical river, this city was founded in the spring of 1420 as a centre of the Hussite revolutionary movement. At first carefully planned, it later developed organically, and the shape of its square reflects this trajectory. Its streets were intentionally designed in zigzag formation, so that enemies would have difficulty reaching the centre. Although it is hard to see in the photograph, the square is sloped, which gives it an additional spatial dimension.

Jindřichův Hradec, Czech Republic
Náměstí Míru

This square takes the shape of an elongated trapezoid, which intersects with the square of the church. The 15th meridian east passes near the square, next to the wall of the Gothic church of the Dormition of the Holy Mother. Its first written mention was in 1220, when Jindřich I built a Gothic castle in an area protected by waterways. A mid-13th century settlement grew as craftsmen started to build improvised buildings around the castle, occasionally holding fairs next to it. The town was originally called Nova Domus in medieval Latin, which led to its German name, Neuhaus. It flourished during the second half of the 16th century, a time when the Gothic houses in the square and nearby streets were redecorated in Renaissance style. Notable among these include the Langer House on the northeastern side, with its façade decorated with Biblical scenes using the *sgraffito* technique, dating from 1579; the City Hall building, with its origins dating back to the Middle Ages, though its current form dates to 1807; and the column of the Holy Trinity, richly decorated with Baroque statues, sculpted by the master craftsman Matthew Strachovský in the second half of the 18th century.

Telč, Czech Republic
Náměstí Zachariáše z Hradce

Founded in 1354, in a thick forest, where two roads crossed near waterways at the border between Moravia, Bohemia and Austria, Telč (or Teltsch in German), had the misfortune of experiencing a great fire two centuries later. The city was quickly rebuilt following the original plan, while integrating the latest in building styles and techniques. The Gothic castle was remade in the Renaissance style and lofts were built for the houses in the square. The houses received painted façades, later replaced in the 18th century with rococo and baroque ones. The medieval Gothic arch on the ground floor remained unchanged. It is continuous, uniting all the houses in the square. Two churches were built and a plague column was dedicated to Saint John Nepomuk, flanked by two fountains.

Towards the end of the 18th century, time suddenly stopped in Telč, with the end of its age of glory and economic development. The city reached our times without further changes – unaffected by industrialisation and, through some miracle, without the construction of socialist blocks. It is straight out of a book of folk tales. The map of the city is practically synonymous with the triangular square. One step beyond it brings you to the yellow canola fields of the Bohemian hills.

Štramberk, Czech Republic
Náměstí

Similar to many other small, out-of-the-way places, this square is simply called 'Square,' or Náměstí in Czech. Štramberk is yet another example of an entire town condensed into its square. Aside from the row of houses that line its perimeter, two or three additional streets complete the map. Trúba, a cylindrical tower consisting of the remains of a castle about which few things are known, dominates the settlement, perched on a nearby wooded hillside. Everything here reminds one of a fairy tale, from the forests to the castle to the square. A large number of wooden houses from the 18th and 19th centuries also add to the local cultural heritage. The land where Štramberk is located is called Valašsko, derived from the name of the populace who migrated here in waves, along the Carpathians from Transylvania and, perhaps, from Bukovina. Though the language of the Vlachs was lost along the way, and these people were slavicised, some customs did survive, such as the traditional building techniques adapted by local Czech and German craftsmen. The wooden houses clearly bring to mind the wooden Romanian architecture from Transylvania. Štramberk has the greatest number of Vlach-style wooden houses, as they are called here, creating an interesting architectural reservation. Its square is also linked to the preparation of local cakes called 'Štramberk ears,' which legally can only be made here. It is said that they have this name because the people of medieval Štramberk thought they resembled the ears of captured Tatar soldiers, during the time of the Tatar raids.

Pelhřimov, Czech Republic
Masarykovo náměstí

Pelhřimov, or Pilgrims in German, houses one of the Czech Republic's largest squares, whose features have remained unchanged since the Middle Ages. Nearly every historical architectural style, from Gothic to the early

functionalism of the First Czechoslovak Republic, can be found here. Following a fire in the 16th century, the Gothic houses were adorned with Renaissance façades. Another fire, in 1766, resulted in some of the façades being rebuilt in Baroque style. The house at Number 17 is one of the most notable examples of the influence of the Italian Renaissance. At the square's centre stands the fountain of Saint Jakob, whose current appearance dates from 1848. It has no plague column, which is atypical for the squares in this region.

Nový Jičín, Czech Republic
Masarykovo náměstí

From its highly regulated structure, it appears that this town was founded at the end of the 13th century, most likely from nothing, on the grounds of a barren field. Its square, with its nearly even sides, includes buildings with very different styles. It has been deemed the most beautiful square north of the Alps, and is surrounded on all sides by arches, constructed in 1503 after a great fire had destroyed the older, mostly wooden houses. The purpose of the arches was to provide shelter for trading stands, and to connect to the entrance of the *mazhaus*, as the large rooms on the ground floor were called. Other fires affected the square in 1768 and 1773, so that the façades were rebuilt in Historicist and Neo-Classical styles in the 19th century. At the centre of the square is a splendid plague column, erected to commemorate the plague of 1680. There is also a statue of Saint Nicholas, protector both of children and

trade, and a fountain called 'the fountain of time,' for the water's movements are synchronised with the clock in the City Hall. Nový Jičín features the oldest hat factory in Europe, and one of the buildings in the square houses a museum dedicated to this history.

Kroměříž, Czech Republic
Velké náměstí

Kroměříž is first mentioned in 1110. It has a large square, whose focal point is a baroque-style column, which marks the end of the plague epidemic in 1680. Next to it there is a fountain, part of the town's water supply, dating from 1665, though modified several times. The City Hall building and a long row of Renaissance style houses and Art Nouveau façades border the square; yet the bishop's palace, with its large and splendid gardens, included on the UNESCO heritage list, is clearly the most impressive of all.

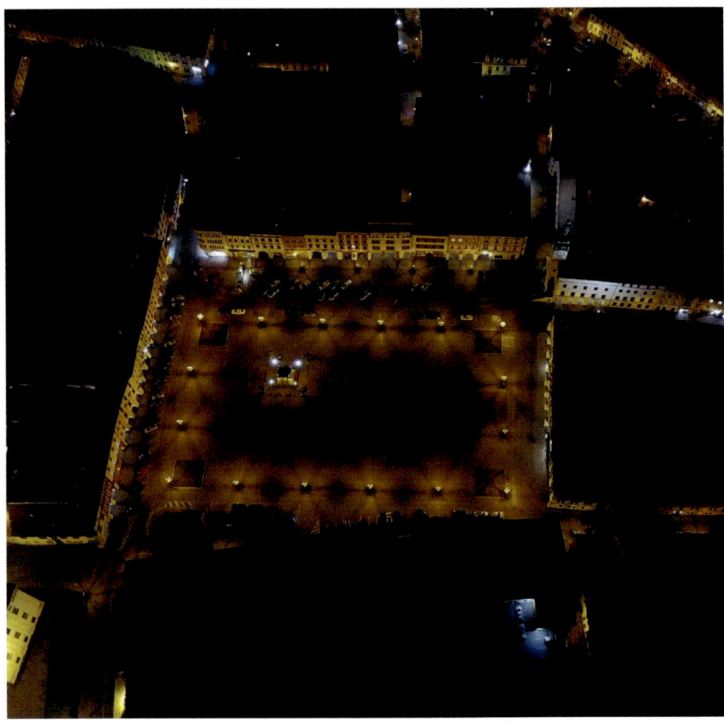

Třeboň, Czech Republic
Masarykovo náměstí

Třeboň, or Wittingau in German, contains one of the best-preserved medieval squares in Bohemia. In fact, only its shape dates from medieval times, since its current form, with its Renaissance and Baroque houses, resulted from the flourishing fish trade of the 14th century. Beginning in the mid-14th century, the natural landscapes around the city were gradually transformed by human intervention. The marshlands gave way to a dense network of over 500 lakes, grouped into sixteen aquatic systems, today a paradise returned to the wilderness and populated with rare species of plants and animals. The largest of these lakes is located close to the city and is tied to the Rosenberg family, owners of the medieval burg. Like all historical cities in Bohemia and Moravia, this square contains a plague column, a Renaissance fountain and a tower building belonging to the City Hall.

It is worth taking a pause from this walk through these squares to look at an unusual phenomenon in urban development known as *synoescism*, which explains some cases where squares that are not centrally located.

Synoecism describes the process of several smaller localities uniting to form a larger one. Aristotle was the first to observe this phenomenon, which translates to 'living together.' It is the equivalent of a political agreement: several communities give up their old status to enter into a self-governing pact. Technological progress was not at the origin of this gesture, but rather the desire to integrate into a polis, meaning a form of democracy.

Most often squares appeared spontaneously in the formerly empty spaces between settlements. Baiasa village, deep in the Pindus Mountains, is said to have formed when four hamlets united. Today's square is in the once empty space between these hamlets.

History has seen some famous cases of *synoecism*. Athens began as a Mycenaean city on the Acropolis. Legend has it that Theseus united this citadel with several surrounding villages, transforming the newly created city into the political capital of the unified Attica. The civic center, the agora, was originally located on the northwest side of the Acropolis. From the 6th century BCE, however, it moved to a more central point of the new alliance: a flat space, located further north, previously a cemetery. The process of Athenian synoecism ended during the Second Peloponnesian War, in 431BCE, when Pericles brought the entire population of Attica inside the walls of Athens.

Athens celebrated its founding story during the feast called *Synoikia*, just as Rome celebrated its synoecism on *Septimontium*. The well-known legend tells how Romulus united the settlement on the Palatine Hill with settlements located on neighboring hills. Historians agree that this event took place in the 8th century BCE. The valley between the hills, previously used by villagers as a place for grazing and as a burial site, was drained and became what history would come to know as the Roman forum.

The formation of Venice presents another famous case of *synoecism*. Venice did not develop around a single centre and, in any case, St. Mark's Square was not this center. In the 7th century, many people sought refuge in the natural isolation of the lagoon from the troubled life that had taken over the cities on the continent in post-Roman times. At that time, the 631 hectares of today's Venice consisted of 124 islands, divided among several independent settlements, each characterised by the existence of a church, a market, a rainwater collection system and at least one canal adjacent to the island. It was not until the 9th century that Venice emerged as a city, when bridges began to connect the islands. The moment was formally marked by the relocation of the doge's palace from the island now called Lido to one of the islets that would become the site of Piazza San Marco. The construction of San Marco was directly related to the slow historical process of *synoecism*, because the appearance of the square, two centuries later, symbolically marked the full unification of the community, now coagulated around a single center.

Memory, says Freud, is structured like a city. The example he gives is Rome, because Rome preserves different layers of past developments. A century later, we can revisit Freud's terms of comparison: a city is like memory; it preserves different layers of past developments. The square is the core of a city's memory.

Košice, Slovakia
Hlavné námestie

The early history of this city and its central square is tied to the German colonists who arrived here in the mid-13th century. The city of Košice (Kaschau in German, Kassa in Hungarian, and Cașovia in the old Romanian chronicles), existed at the crossroads of great trade routes linking the Baltic Sea with the Black Sea; Poland with Transylvania; the east of Europe with the south of Europe. Its urban space is rigorously structured. Three parallel roads run from north to south, with the middle road becoming progressively wider until it meets the main east-west artery, forming a special, lens-shaped square.

The lens shape is due to the construction of this square in a region that formerly functioned as a trade fair. The trade fair took place in a widened section of the road, midway between a castle and an abbey, before any other buildings were constructed. The shape also comes from the unification, through a typical process of a *synoecism*, of two distinct pre-13th century settlements, whose borders were those of the present-day square. At its centre, where these two axes intersect, the German colonists erected a parish church. In the 14th century this church was replaced by the Gothic Cathedral of Saint Elisabeth, the largest Cathedral in Slovakia to this day. The tower of Saint Urban, containing a bell weighing seven tonnes, and the Chapel of Saint Michael, both Gothic and built in the 14th century, flank the Cathedral, creating a unique and unitary whole. The theatre, a Neo-Baroque jewel, was completed in 1899. Gothic houses, Renaissance and Baroque palaces, and Art Nouveau buildings define the perimeter of the square. The lens-shaped square of Košice is the largest and most coherent urban ensemble of its kind, typical of eastern Slovakia.

Podolínec, Slovakia

Mariánske námestie

Podolínec, a town whose name means 'between the hills,' also contains a lens-shaped square, which is not so typical. Interestingly, one side of it closes off suddenly, so it looks like only half a lens. Most likely, its inhabitants originally planned to develop their town further, and widened the walled area, but the development never occurred. Only by comparing it with the other lens-shaped squares in Slovakia can one recognize its features as part of a larger series. Other examples of this type of square include those in neighbouring towns such as Spišská Sobota, now part of Poprad, and Spišská Nová Ves, which contains the largest of all such squares in all of eastern Slovakia. The church in Podolínec's square, dedicated to the Dormition of the Holy Mother, dates from the 13th century. The Renaissance tower was added in 1659 and houses a rare type of bell that was made in 1392. At the northern end of the square is the church of the Piarist monastery.

Bardejov, Slovakia
Radničné námestie

Bardejov square measures 260 by 80 meters. Large and impressive, it is one of the most beautiful squares in Central Europe. Viewed from above, it reveals how the town's historical buildings are divided by a regular network of streets, all adjacent to the square. A well-preserved Jewish Quarter lies between these streets. Bardejov was fortified in 1352. Its structure points to a medieval economic system with urban social structures.

Along three of its sides, 46 two-storey houses with pointed roofs and Renaissance adornments border the square. Typical of the Middle Ages, the houses were built along long narrow plots of land, perpendicular to the square. Saint Egidius Church, at the northern end, first recorded in 1247, dominates the entire town. A 16th century Gothic-Renaissance City Hall building sits at the centre of the square. Statues and a fountain complement the ensemble. Comparing the present-day square with its representation in the 1768 Gáspár plan of the citadel, we can see that no major changes have occurred. Yet this square was not the result of a single construction process; rather, it developed gradually, through a series of additions that stopped only in the 16th century, when the bubonic plague and other calamities blocked its growth and froze the town in time. The original square's structure was not as regular as the present one.

Levoča, Slovakia
Námestie Majstra Pavla

Levoča, called Leutschau in German and Lőcse in Hungarian, was the capital of the historical region of Spiš and features one of the largest squares in Central Europe. It has changed very little over time, with only one or two modern intrusions, bounded by fifty old houses, some with painted façades. At the centre of the rectangular square, which reproduces on a smaller scale the proportions and shape of the still walled burg, one finds the church of Saint Jacob, with the highest carved wooden altar in the world. Made in the late Gothic style, this was the work of a talented and mysterious craftsman named Paul, about whom almost all information was lost during a fire that destroyed the town's archives in 1550. The square nonetheless bears his name today. The Majstra Pavla Square also holds the building of the City Hall whose arches, remade after the fire in 1550, are one of the best examples of Renaissance lay architecture in Slovakia. Finally, one finds a 16th century cage of shame, a form of punishment where the guilty party would be put on public display.

Prešov, Slovakia
Hlavná ulica

This square is called Hlavná ulica, Big Street, because it was formed through the widening of the main road, taking the shape of a lens. It stretches from one end to the other of

the old fortified town, developed by German colonists who were ordered by a 13th century Hungarian king to populate the area after the devastating Mongol invasions. At its centre stands the Gothic church of Saint Nicholas. Beyond the edge of the old town are Socialist apartment buildings. In 1887, a fire destroyed a large number of the houses, so the square's current perimeter contains buildings from the 19th century, although some Gothic, Rococo and Baroque façades did survive the blaze.

Passau, Germany
Domplatz

This urban structure was determined by its geographical position, one of the most spectacular in urban Europe. Passau is situated on a spit of land, at the confluence between the Danube, the Inn and the Ilz, each with differently coloured waters. The Domplatz lies at the highest point of the city, which serves to its advantage, as Passau is threatened by floods every year. The square was built in 1150, and in 1155, after donations by the Bishop Konrad von Babenberg, it became the property of the Cathedral under the condition that clerical houses be built on its free sides. These fourteen buildings were damaged by fire in 1662 and 1680, and then rebuilt by Italian architects in a late Baroque style. In 1824, a statue of Emperor Maximilian I of Bavaria was placed in the square. Thus, for the first time in its history, the square became public, gaining the status of an official town square. It was renovated after 2013. Its pavement was replaced with fine gravel, pointing to its previous historical eras. Its lighting is spectacular, one of the finest in Europe. Highlighting the façade of the Cathedral, leaving the square and the rest of the buildings in semi-shadows, it engages in a subtle game of darkness and light, linking the past, when cities did not have public lighting, with the future. The effect is that of a scene from a Baroque play.

Wismar, Germany
Am Markt

Wismar, a Baltic Sea port, flourished during the 18th and 19th centuries as part of the Hanseatic League. With a size of 10,000 square meters, Am Markt, the city's main square, is one of the largest and most beautiful in northern Germany.

The buildings show a wide variety of styles, from 14th century red brick houses – typical of the late

northern Gothic – to the neoclassical façades or the early 20th century Art Nouveau. The Wasserkunst, a fountain with rich metal decoration brought from the Netherlands in 1602, marks the central point. The viewer may also be impressed by one of the red brick patrician houses, called *Alter Schwede*, which dates back to 1380 and is one of the oldest of its kind.

Bremen, Germany
Marktplatz

During the Middle Ages, Bremen was part of the Hanseatic League, then a Free Imperial City, a status whose official name, Freie Hansestadt Bremen, has been proudly kept by the city to this day. Marktplatz reflects this prosperous past, maintaining its historical character despite the

devastation of the Second World War. The city is the result of transformations during very different epochs, which have nonetheless led to harmonious results: Bremen's square is considered one of the most beautiful in Germany today. Its irregular structure dates to its origins in the Middle Ages. The Rathaus, the Gothic City Hall building, stems from the 15th century, but its façade was adorned at the beginning of the 17th century with one of the finest Renaissance decorations in Europe. St. Petri Dom lies at the city's highest point, positioned obliquely in relation to the square, with its construction beginning in the 13th century. The stone statue of Roland has been a symbol of the city's free status since 1404. Schütting, the 16th century building of the Guilds, became the Chamber of Commerce in 1849. Haus der Bürgershcaft, the concrete and glass building of the local Parliament, was inaugurated in 1966, engaging with the square in an interesting way, as its glass façade reflects the images of the surrounding historical buildings. The statue of the famed Bremen Musicians is on one side of the City Hall, touched by passersby in hopes of having their wishes fulfilled. The red stones of the pavement form the shape of the Hanseatic cross.

Lüneburg, Germany
Platz Am Sande

This city's history is closely linked to its square, which is, in fact, a long and widened street called Am Sande, as it was built on sandy terrain, initially outside the settlement. Am Sande functioned in the past and present as both street and square, competing with and actually surpassing in functionality and liveliness the classical four-sided square containing the Rathaus, or City Hall building.

Lüneburg prospered greatly in the Middle Ages due to the salt trade. The evolution of Am Sande is, from an urbanistic perspective, typical of medieval transformations of former trading spaces at the entrances of citadels, in the cities' central squares, after their fortified areas have been expanded. Am Sande was first documented in 1229 as a settlement connected to the salt mine. This was also where trade routes to Lübeck, Magdeburg, Hamburg and Brunswick passed, and the place quickly became an important trading hub. Trading for salt was conducted at house Number 45, where the old system for loading the salt can still be seen. The most interesting building is Schütting, the beer factory, at the western end of the square. The 108-meter tall spire of the St. John church dominates the square, and a few of its red brick houses – typical of the Hanseatic Baroque period date back to the 14th and 15th centuries.

Schwerin, Germany
Am Markt

Schwerin's Am Markt is the very definition of a square. A quadrangle with nearly equal sides, positioned at the geographical centre of the city, it has held a central role since the beginning, bringing together all the important buildings, from the cathedral to the City Hall, dominated from a distance by a fairy-tale like castle. Strict trading rules, dating back to the time of Henry the Lion, have governed the square so that the city might enjoy economic growth. Each kind of trade had a well-defined place. For instance, fish could only be sold on the northeast side of the square; butchers had to have covered stands; only local traders and craftsmen were allowed to trade their wares in the market. After 1171, foreign merchants were allowed into the city only on specific days of the year.

Stralsund, Germany
Alter Markt, Neuer Markt

The Old Square and the New Square lie at opposite ends of town, almost symmetrically positioned relative to its geographical centre, which is atypical for the Middle Ages. Despite their names, they were probably built not so far apart: Alter Markt was first recorded in 1277, when a document called it a forum, while Neuer Markt was recorded less than a decade later, in 1285. The old square has always had a main role, but the two are similar in many respects, including shape, surface and even function. Isolated among the waters, with red brick Gothic churches, Stralsund is a splendid medieval, Hanseatic town on the Baltic Sea.

Wernigerode, Germany
Marktplatz

This colourful and cheerful City Hall building dates from 1277, when it served as the main offices of a private theatre. In 1427, the building was donated to the city. In its basement were wine cellars, which still exist today. Its current appearance dates back to the 16th century, when a number of fires made it necessary to rebuild the city. In the middle of the square stands a Neo-Gothic fountain from the mid-19th century. Elsewhere, one finds houses with painted woodwork of various colours and sizes. The space has, nonetheless, a well-balanced and uniform appearance.

The origins of European squares can be traced through a continuous historical thread back to Greek antiquity, where the *plateia* and the *agora* appeared. This continuity supports the argument that the urban square is innately European - other cultures, even if they possess squares, indeed some very large in size, lack such ties. The square was invented and developed as an architectural form in Europe, and exported across the world, mainly during the colonial period.

At first a simple widening of the main road in the Greek polis, the square evolved, acquiring over time community and religious functions, which in turn led to formal and aesthetic developments. The *agora* of Miletus, associated with the architect Hippodamus, would become the paradigm for city planning. Destroyed by the Persians in 494 BCE, Miletus was rebuilt according to a regular geometric grid including the agora, conceived of by Hippodamus. From the 5th century BCE onwards, Greeks and Romans built cities according to this plan. Roman architects adopted the Greek square, and the *forum* became essential to spatial planning. After the fall of the Roman Empire, urban life returned to Europe around the year 900CE, with many medieval burgs growing atop the ruins of old Roman settlements, and retaining their plans, with the forum evolving into a central square, as one finds in Zadar or Poreč, on the Dalmatian coast.

Photographing a medieval town from above clearly shows the fundamental opposition between the town's edges and its centre. Medieval towns were invariably surrounded by walls; Some, such as Óbidos, in Portugal, have kept these fortifications intact to the present day. The square is a wide space, standing in volumetric opposition to narrow winding city streets. The medieval square nearly always features a cathedral and a fountain. In smaller towns, the fountain also had a functional role. In larger towns, the fountain was more connected to tradition and ritual, therefore playing a more aesthetic role. The existence of defensive walls had important consequences for the cities of Western Europe. Firstly, for centuries, limited space imposed a population cap within the confines of the walls. When the population grew, it was preferable to build new cities rather than expand the fortified centre, which is why so many new settlements were founded in the Middle Ages. Construction always began from the centre: the square was the first place to be established. A second important consequence of walls was that the centre changed very little, if at all. In medieval communities the square was essentially superimposed on the geometrical centre. It was the most protected space, and the last place to be reached by the enemy. Access to cities was controlled via gates. All entry roads led to the central square. The town walls unequivocally delineate the centre from the periphery. As town walls started to come down at the dawn of modernity, settlements tended to expand concentrically, rather than linearly, adding more space to pre-existing structures, still visible today in many European cities.

Renaissance Europe inherited these medieval cities, but had little love for them, instead searching for a new kind of urban world. The Renaissance era is more renowned for the founding of fictitious cities than of real ones; theory usually gave way to practise only as the result of a calamities. On the 21st of September 1561, a great fire engulfed the city of Valladolid. This catastrophe turned into a blessing for urbanism. Plaza Mayor, still one of the largest squares in Spain today, was built in the cleared space. Although it was the first regular square in Europe, it remains relatively unknown. The architectural and urban pattern instituted at Valladolid became the template for many other squares. This form reached its apex in 1729, with the stunning Plaza Mayor in Salamanca. The aerial photograph reveals that the square's perimeter is not actually rectangular, but a trapezoid. From street level, its sides appear to be even and parallel, but this is a subtle optical illusion, carefully calculated to increase the sense of depth, thus compensating for the relatively small space available to the architect.

Cities continued to be built with fortifications in the 16th century, but the task of city planning increasingly passed from the architect-artist to the tactician-engineer. By the 17th century, Vauban's conceptual star fort marked the height of this paradigm shift, which spread rapidly across Europe, from Naarden and Bourtange, in Holland, to Almeida, in Portugal, to Alba Carolina, in Romania. Vauban's city became a military settlement, capable of stationing large numbers of soldiers within massively fortified city walls. These fortifications have a perfect structure, with straight and rectilinear streets that always lead to a large central square. From the ground, the perfect plan of the forts can only be sensed, lost in the austerity of the buildings, but from above we see stars, settled on the earth, whose core is clearly the central square.

From the mid-18th century and throughout the 19th century, cities reinvented themselves in ways that reflected military, technological, and political changes. The self-governing power of urban communities steadily dwindled and eventually collapsed under the autocracy of monarchs. Aristocrats increasingly migrated from their summer palaces to newly-built urban dwellings in order to be closer to the governing centres. In time, these urban residences became their main homes, and suddenly, a new interest was taken in the city's appearance. If ancient medieval settlements had structures based on the needs of the entire community, new city plans corresponded to the tastes of the aristocracy. Kings brought soldiers into the cities, who in turn required straight streets in order to mobilise swiftly and organise proper parades.

When streets are straightened, a new perspective opens up, the pedestrian can see beyond the first turn. From this it is a small step to theorising the *vista* – urban aesthetics have been forever transformed with the straightening of streets. Unknown in classical Antiquity, the *vista* requires a more complex urban vision: no longer intended to only be seen up close, monuments and statues become landmarks found at the ends of long, straight streets, allowing squares to be seen from afar. A chance effect became a studied technique. Triumphal archways, commemorative columns and statues were meant to be beautiful from a distance as well. The next logical step was the development of ceremonial axes crossing cities, connecting squares. As seen from above, Lisbon unveils the transformations undertaken by the leadership of the Marquis of Pombal, after the devastating earthquake of 1 November 1755. Lisbon's squares represent an interconnected system: broad aligned boulevards link the Trade Square to Rosio, Rosio to de Figueira, Martim Moniz to the Restauradores, the Restauradores to Praça do Marquês de Pombal, each with impressive monuments at their centres.

Goslar, Germany
Marktplatz

Goslar was founded in 920 by Henric I of Germany. Shortly thereafter, silver mines were discovered in the region. For this reason, the Saxon kings moved to Goslar, which precipitated its rapid development. By the 18th century, the mines were exhausted, and the growth suddenly stopped. Goslar has remained intact to this day, having escaped the bombings from the war. Its square is a medieval jewel, featuring the arched City Hall building, the headquarters of the Tailor's Guild, a fountain from the 17th century, and houses with painted woodwork. Beyond the City Hall rise the spires of the church. The pavement, with its brown and grey lines, provides a unified aspect to the mottled display.

Naarden, Netherlands
Markt

There is nothing spectacular about Naarden Square. It is an irregular, not particularly large space, unfolding around Grote Kerk, a red brick church built in the northern Gothic style of the 15th century, having been dedicated to St. Vitius before the Protestant Reformation. Nevertheless, this church is among the oldest in the Netherlands, having survived a fire following the Spanish invasion of 1557. In the square, to one side of the church, lies the statue of Comenius, who was born in Naarden. At one corner of the square is a Renaissance-style City Hall, adorned with allegorical human figures. Even if this square is nothing special, it has a spectacular effect as a whole. Markt is the centre of a star-shaped fort, surrounded by a double row of water ditches.

Elburg, Netherlands

Marktplatz

Elburg's square is the result of an intersection between two main arteries, reproducing on a smaller scale the quadrangular shape of the city. Elburg has perfect geometrical proportions, thought out in such a way that its measurements link to the golden ratio. The city, whose shape has remained unchanged over the years, was built between 1392 and 1396, and is unusual for the Middle Ages, as all of its roads link both to the city's edges and its square, which lies exactly at the geometric centre of the quadrangle.

Bourtange, Netherlands
Marktplein

Today this is a village, with 133 houses and fewer than 300 inhabitants. Yet Bourtange was built as a military fort in 1593, during the Dutch Revolt, on the orders of William the Silent. It held this role until 1851, when it officially lost its defensive function and became populated by craftsmen and farmers. Its initial purpose was to guard the road linking Spanish Groningen to Germany. It is one of the most spectacular star-shaped forts in Europe. Its pentagonal plan and its network of canals and fortifications respect the original project. The square stands in the geometric centre and follows the pentagonal shape of the buildings placed within the fort. Its perimeter is perfectly defined by fourteen lime trees, which are over 300 years old. The square contains the most important houses: the captain's house, the commander's house and the house of the school headmaster – the placement of its buildings was hierarchical. The Protestant church dates from 1869 and, notably, is situated close to the square but not within the square itself.

Amersfoort, Netherlands
Marktplein de Hof

For a city, the centre-margin relation is defining. Amersfoort exceptionally maintains the traces of its successive borders, with the birds-eye view of the city perfectly illustrating this historical relation. The walls surrounding the centre were torn down in the 15th century, but their original positions can still be seen, marked by the *muurhuizen*, or clay wall-houses. Linear suburbs have grown outside the old city, along the main roads. From above, this former boundary can be clearly seen once again. In time, the spaces between these and the city were filled up, and the city itself expanded beyond the highway. At the centre, in the midst of these successive boundaries, stands the square, Marktplein de Hof.

Salamanca, Spain
Plaza Mayor

The construction of this square began in 1729, by order of Phillip V, with the square primarily intended for bullfights. Today, it is seen as one of the most beautiful squares in Spain, as well as in the whole of Europe. The space offers a paradoxical optical illusion. From the ground it appears to be a perfect quadrangle, but when seen from an aerial perspective, the shape is irregular. The baroque façades of the building, which surround and define the square's perimeter, seem perfectly symmetrical at first glance, but in reality, none of them are the same height.

Entire books have been written about this square in Salamanca, and, to this day, it is considered the absolute model of Spanish squares.

Valladolid, Spain
Plaza Mayor

One of the largest in Spain, the Plaza Mayor in Valladolid has a perfectly rectangular shape, with a length of 122 meters and a width of 82 meters, establishing a 3:2 proportion. It is the first square built in Spain by a King: closed, with a regular plan. It served as a model for the central square in Madrid, built in 1617, and the one in Salamanca, built in 1729, where the Valladolid

architectural and urban pattern reached its perfection. A long series of squares in Spain and South America were inspired by the latter two, thus indirectly pointing to the square in Valladolid.

On the 21st of September 1561, a fire engulfed Valladolid and burned for three days. The disaster became an opportunity to apply new urban ideas. The plan of the new square followed the principles of Renaissance balance and symmetry. The square was conceived as a closed, rectangular space, completely hollow in the middle, with entrances through porticoes. The architect Francisco de Salamanca projected identical, mirrored façades. Behind them are living areas for functionaries and guild members. A colonnade spans the level of the street.

Peñafiel, Spain
Plaza del Coso

Peñafiel is more renowned for its wines and the massive medieval castle that dominates this settlement than for its square, but Plaza del Coso is nonetheless very interesting from a historical and urbanistic perspective. It is a very large square – 3500 square meters in size – unpaved, and surrounded by 48 houses, all with suspended wooden balconies. Those still standing today date from the 18th and 19th centuries, but the square essentially looked

the same in the Middle Ages. In the summer, during the celebration of San Roque, bullfighting is organised here. On Easter Sunday, the Descent of the Angel ceremony is held here. The buildings are privately owned, but the balconies have always been considered public property, and are used on such occasions for watching the spectacles and rituals in the square. Plaza del Coso was originally intended as an entertainment arena – unusual for the Middle Ages. Neither the City Hall nor the cathedral are located here. However, chronologically speaking, it is considered one of the first *plaza major* examples in Spain.

Ávila, Spain
Plaza del Mercado Chico

It is said that the Roman *forum* once stood on the site of the Plaza del Mercado, which became the centre of the community at the end of the 11th century when the region was repopulated. In the Middle Ages, this was a *plaza porticada*, a square bordered by columns, with a weekly fair, as well as regular corridas and religious ceremonies. The square was the site of royal receptions but also beheadings. In the 15th century, in front of the San Juan church, in the presence of Torquemada, converted Jews were burnt at the stake. Plaza del Mercado Chico is an interesting case representing the fight between secular and religious power. The existence of the San Juan church on the southern side of the square resulted in the church claiming half of it. In the end, the city council voted for building a regular square in 1770. The construction was slow going and only finalised in 1870, with a line of columns masking San Juan, and transforming Plaza del Mercado Chico into a City Hall square.

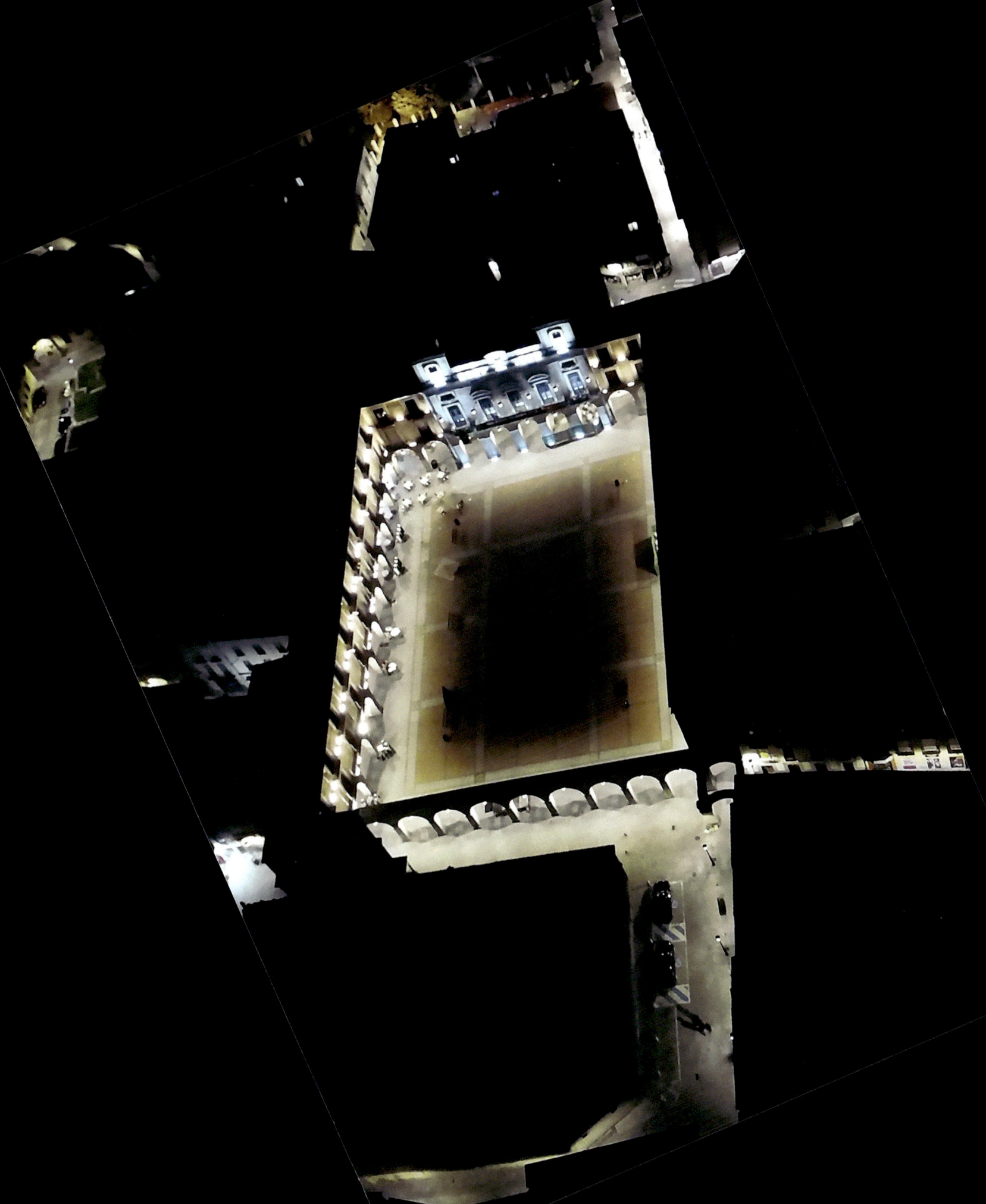

Bilbao, Spain
Plaza Nueva

This is a square filled with life, bars, shops, taverns, terraces, restaurants. Built between 1821 and 1851 in a neoclassical style and surrounded by identical buildings, featuring three levels and a colonnade, it is called Plaza Nueva, in contrast to the city's medieval square, and measures 3400 square meters. The functionalist style of its buildings and the absence of rich decoration reflect the ideas of the Enlightenment, for the square was planned at the end of the 18th century, although its construction bdid not begin until a few decades later. The first architect of the square was Silvestre Pérez. The space gives one the feeling of a giant yet intimate palace salon. Every Sunday, Plaza Nueva hosts a flea market.

Chinchón, Spain

Plaza Mayor

Adapting a square according to its functions can sometimes lead to unpredictable forms. The Chinchón Plaza Mayor, not far from Madrid, has an elliptical shape and an unpaved centre. Along its sides, identical three-storey buildings from the 15th and 17th centuries feature porches that lead directly to the square. There are no fewer than 234 wooden galleries in total. The square lies at the centre of the village, sitting at its lowest point. Wherever one comes from, one must descend to reach this square, and every house has a view of it. In Spain, squares have often served as improvised bullrings. But in Chinchón, this square had such a purpose from the start. Along with its two corridas, it serves many other functions, including hosting traditional festivals (the village has a choir), religious ceremonies during the *Semana Santa*, weekly fairs and games of all kinds. It even functions as a weekend dance arena. In the past, it was the site of public executions. But it has also been a film set: scenes from *Around the World in Eighty Days* (1956) were shot here, an occasion for the entire population of this tiny settlement to serve as extras.

Frías, Spain
Plaza Mayor

Frías has been proudly wearing the title of town ever since 1435. It is considered the smallest town in Spain today. Perched spectacularly on a rock, Frías had no space to grow, and therefore its size remained always the same. But even such a small space has a square, as the town's map shows… two streets. Naturally, one street leads up to the base of the castle in the square, and the other street, back. The mere fact that a miniature town has a Playa Mayor speaks of the communal importance of this space for Spanish settlements. The Plaza Mayor is an architectural space, but especially an anthropological one, for the entire life of the community takes place here.

Plasencia, Spain
Plaza Mayor

This historic town has Plaza Mayor at its nucleus, with its streets radiating out, to the gates and away from the citadel, whose walls have been well kept to this day. The City Hall building, dating from the 16th century, is known for *El abuelo Mayorga*, a funny human figurine who, every half hour, strikes the building's bell with his hammer. This figure has become the symbol of the town, with many real and imagined tales linked to it. Of different heights, built in different epochs and in different styles, tthe buildings that define the square's perimeter comprise an imposing whole, with an unexpectedly unified personality. Plaza Mayor in Plasencia is one of the least known, but still very beautiful squares in Spain.

Segovia, Spain
Plaza Mayor

Segovia's Plaza Mayor has a historical significance for Spain as the location of Queen Isabella of Castile's coronation in 1474, when it was still known as Plaza de San Miguel. This otherwise typical Spanish square offers an unexpected visual 'twist' from an urbanistic point of view: a massive cathedral, one of the last Gothic structures built in Europe, occupies one end of the square. But Plaza Mayor manages not to be overshadowed by the cathedral; instead, through a play on perspective, it scales the structure down to a more intimate human height.

Cáceres, Spain

Plaza Mayor

This is one of the largest squares in Spain and lies right at the entrance of the medieval town. Its originated in the 11th century, when the space was used for the great traditional holidays. The buildings stem from different eras, all of them with 16th century ground floor colonnade. On the northwestern side, the Bujaco Tower is an eye-catching building, now a symbol of the city. It was built during the Arab rule, on top of Roman foundations. The origins of its name may come from the local word for straw dolls, *bujacos*.

Ciudad Rodrigo, Spain
Plaza Mayor

This town took its name from Count Rodrigo González Girón, who, in the mid-12th century, banished the Moors from this region once and for all, and built this town on top of a former Roman castrum, itself built atop a Celtic settlement. Its solid fortifications speak to its position on the border with Portugal. Paradoxically, although it is one of the most well-defended European borders on both sides, this frontier was the most stable in all of Europe's history and has remained this way for 500 years. The only fighting to take place here was against Napoleon's armies. Nowhere is the relationship between centre and periphery more marked than in such citadels.

Almeida, Portugal
Praça de São João

On the Portuguese side of the border there are even more fortifications than on the Spanish side. Almeida is located in the north of Portugal. It is a star-shaped fort with twelve Vauban style corners, built in 1641. The Spanish only entered there once in all their history, and then with the help of the French. The square is an irregular quadrilateral and is not positioned quite geometrically. While the star is not perfect, its role as a centre is obvious when viewed in relation to the margins of the citadel.

Tomar, Portugal
Praça da República

Beneath this city's pavement lies a Roman settlement, but Tomar was founded after the expulsion of the Moors, in the 12th century. It is not certain whether the square served as a replacement for the Roman *forum*, as was the case nearly everywhere in Europe, including many cities in Portugal. However this seems unlikely given Tomar's unique history and geography. The area is shrouded in legends and mysticism. Tomar was founded by Gualdim Pais (whose statue stands in the square), the leader of the Knights Templar, and it is believed that he did not choose the site by chance. Gualdim Pais first built a monastery and a castle, which stands to this day on a hill bordering the square. The São João Baptista church and the City Hall stand along the shorter sides of the square, with its remaining sides featuring houses from the 17th century.

Óbidos, Portugal
Praça de Santa Maria

Óbidos is the stereotypical portrait of a medieval city: a closed world, a world onto itself, hierarchical, assembled around a centre, marked by its square and its Cathedral, a settlement surrounded by walls.

Óbidos is one of the few medieval settlements whose original walls are still intact. Praça de Santa Maria contains its most important buildings: the Casa da Picota, dating from the 15th century, a vertical fountain, an old covered square and, of course, the Igreja de Santa Maria, renowned as the site of Alfonso V's marriage to Isabella, his eight-year-old cousin.

Lisbon, Portugal
Praça de D. Pedro IV

Although its official name is Praça de D. Pedro IV, this square is known by locals as Rossio. The site of many important historical events, it has been considered the heart of Lisbon since the Middle Ages. Around 1450, Paço dos Estaus was built on the northern side of the square, on the grounds of the existing theatre.

The palace was originally used for hosting foreign dignitaries. It then became a seat of the Inquisition, and, as a result, Rossio was for many years a place of public executions. Its current look is largely due to its renovations planned by the Marquise of Pombal after the earthquake of 1755, coordinated by architects Eugénio dos Santos and Carlos Mardel. Its splendid pavement, a typical Portuguese mosaic, dates from the 19th century. A statue of King Pedro IV stands atop the central column, built in 1874, giving the square its official name.

Lisbon, Portugal
Praça do Comércio

This square owes its existence to a great earthquake that took place on 1 November 1755, and the subsequent fire. A new, well-ordered city emerged from the ruins, the result of reconstruction efforts coordinated by the Marquise of Pombal, the leader of the royal government.

Praça do Comércio was built on Terreiro de Paço, the site of the old courtyard of the Royal Palace. This name is still used for the square, with one side facing the Tejo, the greatest river on the Iberian Peninsula. Measuring 175 by 180 meters, this square is one of the largest on the European continent.

Lisbon, Portugal
Praça do Município

At a short distance from the monumental Praça do Comércio stands the municipal square, which hosts three important buildings: the Municipality, the Court of Appeals and the Naval Arsenal. It is a small, quiet square, with different rhythms from the Praça do Comércio, which, following the Rua do Arsenal, stands less than 70 meters ahead. Praça do Município is equally part of the urban fabric woven from the city's reconstruction under the guidance of the Marquise of Pombal. This historical detail is enough to make it clear that they must be understood as counterpoints, that is, as parts of a broader, interconnected system of squares.

A square can be perceived to exist on at least several planes: architectural, historical, social, symbolic. The latter follows a unique set of rules to materialise out of elements from the other planes.

A square is an architectural space. Like any architectural space, the square is finite: it has edges. The buildings that delimit it, define the square. Therefore, spatially speaking, the buildings in a square are the square. Consequence? A square is born when a series of buildings establish a perimeter and, implicitly, define the centre of a settlement (or the centre of some part of a settlement). It is less important, from this point of view, if buildings are replaced – the square begins to exist with the first constructions that define it. In 1063, Piazza San Marco was born with the construction of the first basilica. Although the year is unknown, the planting of plane trees of Kallarites and Syrrako marked the birth of the squares as well as, of course, the settlements.

However, buildings alone do not a square make. In order to exist as an architectural and geometric space, a square is necessarily and *a priori* an anthropological space. It can exist after, but not outside of the history of the community that built it. The physical square generates a square of the people who live in it, pass through it, who make it the backdrop of their daily lives, make it part of their individual and, especially, collective histories. In this sense, buildings are not the square, but are in the square – situated within a space that contains them, as if the square exists beyond the walls. Looking at present day Lisbon from above illustrates how a city preserves the records of its inhabitants' evolving relationship to space, time and the world, through different approaches to construction, such as the stark contrast between the regular structures of the 18th century juxtaposed with the chaotic medieval city that survived the great earthquake of 1755.

The symbolic square emerges from the interactions between the architectural and anthropological planes of a physical square. These interactions are a natural 'chemical reaction' that takes place in any human settlement. The emerging symbolic square is at first codependent on the underlying planes – all these layers are superimposed. But with time they drift apart, and the symbolic square distills into an abstract form, a meaningful symbol that refracts back onto the concrete physical square, even though its genesis derives from the latter, which in a sense metaphysically results from a community's designs, plans, and constructions. In short, a certain 'sum' of the parts takes on a new value that then imposes itself upon the parts that comprised it.

In order for a square to exist, structures alone do not suffice. Cities are a blend of people and buildings, and the relation between these disparate elements is not as straightforward as it would seem at first glance. People create buildings, but the ways in which a community sets its story, history, religion, beliefs, and concrete needs of daily life into a space have remained unclear to this day. The nuances of this complicated process are elusive, and will most likely never be fully understood.

A square consists of its architecture, but, at the same time, it is much more than its architecture alone. Its entire past, chained to an invisible-visible system of links to the symbolic imaginary of the community, makes its presence strongly felt in the existence of the square.

Coimbra, Portugal
Praça 8 de Maio

Coimbra is famous for its university, and monumental squares are located in the university area. The city also possesses a small jewel of a square, modest in size but convincing through its balanced proportions and its historical importance. It is Praça 8 de Maio, found in the city centre, in front of the Santa Cruz Monastery, while further on one finds the Câmara Municipal. This small space manages to avoid being dwarfed by the height and splendour of the Manueline façade of the church where the first two kings of Portugal lie buried. The buildings on the other three sides are just as visible; likewise the central fountain. The contemporary redesign of the square also contributes to its feeling of openness.

Leiria, Portugal
Praça Francisco Rodrigues Lobo

Filled with cafes and terraces, and host to numerous events, Praça Lobo plays an important role in the social and economic life of Leiria. Seasonal fairs in this square go as far back as the Middle Ages. Its pavement design is renowned throughout Portugal.

Elvas, Portugal
Praça da República

Elvas lies at the southern end of the Portuguese-Spanish border, in the province of Portalegre. It dates from the 17th century and is one of the finest Vauban fortifications. Resisting a number of Spanish sieges, in 1644, 1659, 1711 and 1801, it proved unconquerable. The square's construction began in 1511. Here, the Nossa Senhora da Assunção Church was built, which was subsequently raised to the rank of Cathedral. Of note is the surrounding pavement, with its grey tones, forming patterns of optical illusions.

Content

EUROPEAN SQUARES
and their histories — 5

Pienza, Italy
Piazza Pio II — 8

Gubbio, Italy
Piazza Grande — 10

Todi, Italy
Piazza del Popolo
Piazza Garibaldi — 12

Vicenza, Italy
Piazza dei Signori
Piazza delle Biade
Piazza delle Erbe
Piazzetta Palladio — 14

16   Brescia, Italy
Piazza Paolo VI
Piazza della Loggia

18   Pitigliano, Italy
Piazza San Gregorio VII

20   Arezzo, Italy
Piazza Grande

22   Città di Castello, Italy
Piazza Gabriotti
Piazza Matteotti

24   Lucca, Italy
Piazza dell'Anfiteatro

26   Bergamo, Italy
Piazza Vechia
Piazza Duomo

28   Orvieto, Italy
Piazza del Duomo

Assisi, Italy Piazza del Comune	30
Marostica, Italy Piazza Castello	32
Udine, Italy Piazza della Libertà	34
Palmanova, Italy Piazza Grande	36
Trieste, Italy Piazza dell'Unità d'Italia	38
The Lives of European Squares	40
Venice, Italy Piazza San Marco	42

44 Piran, Slovenia
Tartinijev trg

46 Ljubljana, Slovenia
Prešernov trg
Mestni trg

48 Rovinj, Croatia
Trg Svete Eufemije
Trg G. Matteottija

50 Split, Croatia
Trg Peristil

52 Dubrovnik, Croatia
Trg Luža
Gundulićeva poljana

54 Zadar, Croatia
Trg Rimskog Foruma

56 Motovun, Croatia
Trg Andrea Antico

Trogir, Croatia
Trg Ivana Pavla II   58

Poreč, Croatia
Trg Marafor   60
Trg Slobode

Šibenik, Croatia
Trg Republike Hrvatske   62

Kotor, Montenegro
Trg od Oružja
Trg od Brašna   64
Pjaca Svetog Tripuna
Trg Sveti Luke

Herceg Novi, Montenegro
Trg Herceg Stjepana   66

Perast, Montenegro
Trg Sveti Nikole   68

Kruševo, Republic of
North Macedonia   70
Cearshia

72   Etymologies

74   Istanbul, Turkey
Sultanahmet Meydanı

76   Tbilisi, Georgia
Meidan Bazaar

78   Tbilisi, Georgia
Tavisuplebis Moedani

80   Sarajevo,
Bosnia and Herzegovina
Baščaršija

82   Thessaloniki, Greece
Plateia Aristotelous

84   Kallarites, Greece
Plateia

Syrrako, Greece
Plateia — 86

Vovousa, Greece
Plateia — 88

The squares of Aromanian Settlements from The Pindus Mountains, Greece — 90

Sofia, Bulgaria
Ploshcead Sveti Aleksandar Nevski — 96

Tryavna, Bulgaria
Ploshchead Kapitan Diado Nikola — 98

Bucharest, Romania
Piața Universității — 100

Brașov, Romania
Piața Sfatului — 102

104   Sibiu, Romania
Piața Mare
Piața Mică

106   Alba Iulia, Romania
Piața Cetății

108   Timișoara, Romania
Piața Unirii
Piața Libertății
Piața Victoriei

110   Tarnów, Poland
Rynek

112   Krakow, Poland
Rynek Główny

114   Retz, Austria
Hauptplatz

116   Mikulov, Czech Republic
Náměstí

Znojmo, Czech Republic
 Masarykovo náměstí 118
 Horní náměstí

České Budějovice, Czech Republic 120
Náměstí Přemysla Otakara II

Slavonice, Czech Republic 122
Náměstí Míru
Horní náměstí

Český Krumlov, Czech Republic 124
Náměstí Svornosti

Tábor, Czech Republic 126
Žižkovo náměstí

Jindřichův Hradec, Czech Republic 128
Náměstí Míru

Telč, Czech Republic 130
Náměstí Zachariáše z Hradce

132 Štramberk,
Czech Republic
Náměstí

134 Pelhřimov,
Czech Republic
Masarykovo náměstí

136 Nový Jičín, Czech Republic
Masarykovo náměstí

138 Kroměříž, Czech Republic
Velké náměstí

140 Třeboň, Czech Republic
Masarykovo náměstí

142 Synoecism

144 Košice, Slovakia
Hlavné námestie

Podolínec, Slovakia
Mariánske námestie — 146

Bardejov, Slovakia
Radničné námestie — 148

Levoča, Slovakia
Námestie Majstra Pavla — 150

Prešov, Slovakia
Hlavná ulica — 152

Passau, Germany
Domplatz — 154

Wismar, Germany
Am Markt — 156

Bremen, Germany
Marktplatz — 158

160	Lüneburg, Germany Platz Am Sande	
162	Schwerin, Germany Am Markt	
164	Stralsund, Germany Alter Markt, Neuer Markt	
166	Wernigerode, Germany Marktplatz	
168	Short History of European Squares	
172	Goslar, Germany Marktplatz	
174	Naarden, Netherlands Markt	

Elburg, Netherlands Marktplatz	176
Bourtange, Netherlands Marktplein	178
Amersfoort, Netherlands Marktplein de Hof	180
Salamanca, Spain Plaza Mayor	182
Valladolid, Spain Plaza Mayor	184
Peñafiel, Spain Plaza del Coso	186
Ávila, Spain Plaza del Mercado Chico	188

190 Bilbao, Spain
     Plaza Nueva

192 Chinchón, Spain
     Plaza Mayor

194 Frías, Spain
     Plaza Mayor

196 Plasencia, Spain
     Plaza Mayor

198 Segovia, Spain
     Plaza Mayor

200 Cáceres, Spain
     Plaza Mayor

202 Ciudad Rodrigo, Spain
     Plaza Mayor

Almeida, Portugal
Praça de São João — 204

Tomar, Portugal
Praça da República — 206

Óbidos, Portugal
Praça de Santa Maria — 208

Lisbon, Portugal
Praça de D. Pedro IV — 210

Lisbon, Portugal
Praça do Comércio — 212

Lisbon, Portugal
Praça do Município — 214

The Symbolic Square — 216

218	Coimbra, Portugal Praça 8 de Maio	
220	Leiria, Portugal Praça Francisco Rodrigues Lobo	
222	Elvas, Portugal Praça da República	
240	Bibliography and Credits Acknowledgments	

The complete bibliography forming the basis of this book is extensive, given the subject matter, and listed here it would cover too many additional pages in a book that has another purpose. This bibliography includes both general and specialised works, with numerous volumes dedicated to specific squares, and was consulted for the author's PhD in Architecture. Even if sources are not specified in particular instances, most of the technical data regarding various squares' dimensions, the dates of their construction, etc. are taken primarily from two volumes: Sophie Wolfrum (ed.), Squares. Urban Spaces in Europe, Birkhäuser, Basel, Switzerland, 2015; Paul Zucker, Town and Square. From the Agora to the Green Village, Columbia University Press, USA, 1959. Additional data have also been extracted from the following three volumes: Maria Teresa Feraboli, City Squares of the World, White Star Publishers, Verecelli, Italy, 2007; Robert F. Gatje, Great Public Squares. An Architect's Selection, Norton, New York, London, 2010; Michael Webb, The City Square. A Historical Evolution, Watson-Guptill, New York, USA, 1990.

I am grateful to all those who have contributed, over time and in various forms, to the development of my project on European squares. The project began as research for my PhD, which was followed by conference presentations on the topic; an exhibition presented in several European countries; the production of a film essay; the publication of a book in Romanian; and, now, the publication of this volume in English. Consistent and constant support was necessary for making all of these things possible. In the case of this book, my special thanks go to Carmen Dobrotă, for help given with the travel necessary to realize its images; to Dan Bora, for his patience with reading and borrowing from the text; and to Alyssa Grossman, for her care in proofreading the English version. The project has had a long series of steadfast friends: my PhD coordinator Sorin Vasilescu; Sergiu Singer; Radu Comșa; Dan Lăcătuș; Carmen Constantin; Cristina Rusiecki; Teodora Olteanu; Ricardo Borja Soria Cáceres; Cezar Petre Buiumaci; and, of course, my Mother. Many names are missing, friends to whom I apologize for not having had the space to include them here. Sometimes even the slightest assistance, for example, from a stranger whose name I have forgotten, but who helped me charge the drone's batteries, was essential in obtaining a good photograph. (Cătălin D. Constantin)

CĂTĂLIN D. CONSTANTIN is a book publisher and anthropologist. He teaches Anthropology at the Faculty of Letters, University of Bucharest. His first PhD thesis, published in 2013, focused on everyday life in Romanian cities at the beginning of the 20th century. His second PhD, completed in 2014, a cultural and anthropological reading of urban squares of European cities, was awarded by the *Ion Mincu* University of Architecture and Urbanism. It was the first time that the University of Architecture in Bucharest gave a PhD with the maximum grade to a person who is not an architect by profession.

Cătălin has edited a number of literature collections and photography books dedicated to cultural heritage. For the books he edits, he often produces both text and graphics, considering the combination between these two components essential. *Windows from Bucharest and their stories* sold out in three weeks and reached 1st place in book sales in Romania.

He conducts anthropological field research in the Pindus Mountains of Greece, where he studies the communities of Vlachs, speakers of a neo-Latin idiom on the verge of extinction. For his research he received an honorary diploma from the Macedoromanian Cultural Association, on the occasion of the 140th anniversary of its founding.

He has received the medal of honor awarded by KulturForum Europa, a German Foundation founded by Vice-Chancellor Hans-Dietrich Genscher.

For over five years he has coordinated a series of weekly museum education conferences at the Suțu Palace in Bucharest, Bucharest City Museum.

He has also organized multiple photography exhibitions in Romania, Spain, Turkey, Bulgaria, Azerbaijan, Georgia, Poland, Greece, Ireland, Italy and Portugal.